## FEBRUARY

| M | T | W | T | F | S | S |
|---|---|---|---|---|---|---|
| 1 | 2 | 3 | 4 | 5 | 6 | 7 |
| 8 | 9 | 10 | 11 | 12 | 13 | 14 |
| 15 | 16 | 17 | 18 | 19 | 20 | 21 |
| 22 | 23 | 24 | 25 | 26 | 27 | 28 |

## APRIL

| M | T | W | T | F | S | S |
|---|---|---|---|---|---|---|
|   |   |   | 1 | 2 | 3 | 4 |
| 5 | 6 | 7 | 8 | 9 | 10 | 11 |
| 12 | 13 | 14 | 15 | 16 | 17 | 18 |
| 19 | 20 | 21 | 22 | 23 | 24 | 25 |
| 26 | 27 | 28 | 29 | 30 |   |   |

## JUNE

| M | T | W | T | F | S | S |
|---|---|---|---|---|---|---|
|   | 1 | 2 | 3 | 4 | 5 | 6 |
| 7 | 8 | 9 | 10 | 11 | 12 | 13 |
| 14 | 15 | 16 | 17 | 18 | 19 | 20 |
| 21 | 22 | 23 | 24 | 25 | 26 | 27 |
| 28 | 29 | 30 |   |   |   |   |

# THE
# ALMANAC

## A SEASONAL GUIDE TO
## 2021

### LIA LEENDERTZ

With illustrations by Helen Cann

MITCHELL BEAZLEY

This edition is dedicated to the Gypsy, Romani and Traveller community of Britain and Ireland. A donation has been made to Friends, Families and Travellers, a charity that works and campaigns to end racism against the community and to protect the right to pursue a nomadic way of life. You can support their work at gypsy-traveller.org or follow them on Twitter, @GypsyTravellers.

An Hachette UK Company
www.hachette.co.uk

First published in Great Britain in 2020 by Mitchell Beazley,
an imprint of Octopus Publishing Group Ltd
Carmelite House, 50 Victoria Embankment, London EC4Y 0DZ
www.octo

Text copy
Design an
Illustratio
Music cop

Rasher pu
Samphire
Sugared d

ISBN 978-1
A CIP catalogue record for this book is available from the British Library.
Printed and bound in the United Kingdom
10 9 8 7 6 5 4 3 2 1

Publishing Director: Stephanie Jackson
Creative Director: Jonathan Christie
Designer: Matt Cox at Newman+Eastwood
Editor: Ella Parsons
Data input: Rowan Simpson
Copy Editor: Alison Wormleighton
Senior Production Manager: Peter Hunt

Ovens should be preheated to the specific temperature – if using a fan-assisted oven, follow your oven manufacturer's instructions for adjusting the time and the temperature. Pepper should be freshly ground black pepper unless otherwise stated.

# CONTENTS

# INTRODUCTION

Welcome to *The Almanac: a Seasonal Guide to 2021*. If you are new to *The Almanac*, then welcome, and if you are a regular reader, then hello! This almanac is about celebrating the unfolding year. The old dependables that I include every year are back: moon phases, sunrises and sets, tide timetables and the sky at night. As ever, there are recipes and gardening tips, too, as well as a bit of folklore, nature and a song for each month.

This year's edition has a theme: movement, migration and pilgrimage. This was not a reaction to the unsettling events of 2020 – it was half-written by the time COVID-19 hit – but writing it from lockdown did give me a heightened appreciation of the way in which Britain and Ireland have always been, and continue to be, places of movement and are intimately connected to the rest of the world. Lockdown didn't stop the humpback whales from dropping in on the Firth of Forth during their epic journey from Norway to the Caribbean, or the painted lady butterflies from flitting through our gardens on their strange endless migration. For each month you will find migration tales and a pilgrimage – some ancient, some current, all underlining the spiritual benefits of putting one foot in front of the other. I have investigated the old Romani names for each month and included Romani recipes, to pay homage to these nomads and their seasonal routes. Each month begins with a scene of traditional, seasonal Romani life, as depicted by this year's illustrator, Helen Cann. For every month I have included a method of navigating using the stars, sun or moon, and our monthly folk songs are all shanties this year, work songs with movement at their very heart.

We are all eager to move after so much time cooped up, but this edition is particularly for those for whom staying in was not so different, who were never going to climb mountains anyway. I hope this almanac helps you to travel in your mind all year long, via the swift that flies past your window, through a rasher pudding cooked in the Romani style, and by way of a song of derring-do on the ocean waves. Have a wonderful 2021.

Lia Leendertz

# NOTES ON USING *THE ALMANAC*

### Geographical and cultural scope

The geographical scope of this almanac covers Britain and Ireland. The cultural scope is the stories, songs, food, travels and festivities of all of the people who live within them. I have focused on the nomadic people of Britain and Ireland, their names for the months and their seasonal traditions. There are several distinct groups of travelling people within Britain and Ireland including Irish Travellers and Romanies, though they regularly come together for horse fairs. Although figures do vary, it is estimated that there are more than 200,000 Romanies and Travellers living in the UK today. Sadly the names of the months in many of the traveller languages have been lost, but I was able to track down those once used by Romanies, and so the Romani are the focus of these sections.

### The sky at night

The events within the sky at night section generally fall into three categories: eclipses, meteor showers, and close approaches of the moon to a naked-eye planet, or of two naked-eye planets to each other. While the first two categories are self-explanatory, the third will benefit from a little clarification. The naked-eye planets are those planets that can be easily seen with the naked eye. They are generally very bright, as bright as the brightest stars, and this makes them relatively easy to spot, even in cities where sky-spotting conditions are not ideal. From brightest to dimmest they are: Venus, Jupiter, Mars and Saturn. Those not included in this almanac are Mercury, Neptune and Uranus. Mercury is very hard to spot because it is close to the sun and therefore is usually lost in its glare. Neptune and Uranus can only be spotted with strong telescopes.

A 'close approach' means that two of them, or one of them plus the moon, are in the same part of the sky. They are, of course, nowhere near each other in reality, but to us, looking up, they appear as if they are. This can make them easier to spot than they would be when they are lone-ranging across the sky. To identify the part of the sky where they will most easily be seen, I have given the best time to spot them, plus a compass point and the altitude. The time is important because the sky wheels around us as the night wears on. The altitude is given in degrees: the horizon is 0 degrees and straight up is 90 degrees.

### Tides

A full tide timetable is given each month for Dover, because Dover is widely used as a standard port from which to work out all other tides. The table below shows how you can make it work for elsewhere. Add or subtract these amounts of time from the tide you are interested in on the monthly table, and you will have the tide time for your particular location. For instance, if it is high tide at Dover at midday, it will be high tide at Bristol (–4h 10m) at 07.50 and at London Bridge (+2h 52m) at 14.52. All times have been adjusted for British Summer Time (BST) and Irish Standard Time (IST).

If your local port or beach is not featured here, just search online for 'tide differences on Dover', plus the name of your chosen spot. Note that these approximations provide a fairly rough idea of tide times, though they will be correct within ten minutes or so.

| Aberdeen: | +2h 31m | Cork: | –5h 23m |
|---|---|---|---|
| Firth of Forth: | +3h 50m | Swansea: | –4h 50m |
| Port Glasgow: | +1h 32m | Bristol: | –4h 10m |
| Newcastle-upon-Tyne: | +4h 33m | London Bridge: | +2h 52m |
| Belfast Lough: | +0h 7m | Lyme Regis: | –4h 55m |
| Hull: | –4h 52m | Newquay: | –6h 4m |
| Liverpool: | +0h 14m | St Helier, Jersey: | –4h 55m |

Do not use these where accuracy is critical; instead, you will need to buy a local tide timetable, or subscribe to Easy Tide www.ukho.gov.uk/easytide. Also note that no timetable will take into account the effects of wind and barometric pressure.

Spring tide and neap tide dates are also included. Spring tides are the most extreme tides of the month – the highest and lowest – and neap tides the least extreme. Spring tides happen as a result of the pull that occurs when the sun, moon and earth are aligned. Alignment occurs at new moon and full moon, but the surge – the spring tide – is slightly delayed because of the mass of water to be moved. It usually follows one to three days after. Knowledge of spring tides is particularly useful if you are a keen rock-pooler, beachcomber or mudlark. You want a low spring tide for best revelations.

### Gardening by the moon

Just as the moon moves the earth's water to create the tides, some believe that it has other effects on the natural world. If it can move oceans, perhaps it can move ground water, too, and even the water trapped in each plant. Planting by the moon is a method of gardening that taps into the moon's phases. A new moon is considered a good time to sow root crops and those that are slow to germinate, because soil moisture is steadily increasing. Faster-germinating plants that crop above ground should be sown in the run-up to full moon, when the pull is strongest and so ground water is at its highest. The full moon is also the best time to harvest crops for immediate use, as they are at their juiciest. After that, the moon's pull starts to wane and ground water drops – these are good times for pruning (to minimise sap loss), and harvesting for storage (skins are drier and tougher). This almanac makes no claims on the efficacy of planting by the moon, but if you would like to give it a try, the relevant dates and jobs are included for each month. Note that these jobs are not seasonally adjusted and are certainly not an instruction to do every job mentioned every month.

### Songs

This year's folk songs are all shanties. The music and words have been compiled by composer Richard Barnard from a variety of sources, but in the spirit of folk songs he has also put his own spin and interpretation on them.

JANUARY

IVES KERO

MONTH OF THE SNOWS

I

# January

**1** New Year's Day – bank holiday, England, Scotland, Wales, Northern Ireland, Republic of Ireland

**2** Bank holiday, Scotland

**5** Twelfth Night (Christian)

**6** Epiphany/Three Kings' Day/Little Christmas (Christian)

**6** Nollaig na mBan or Women's Christmas (Christian/Irish tradition)

**6** Orthodox Christmas Eve (Orthodox)

**7** Orthodox Christmas Day (Orthodox)

**7** Lidat (Rastafarian)

**11** Plough Monday (English tradition)

**13** Lohri (Punjabi winter festival)

**25** Burns Night (Scottish tradition)

# ROMANI NAME FOR THE MONTH

### Iveskero – month of the snows

Since the 16th century, following their migration from contintenal Europe, there have been Romani families and communities living in the UK. Romani, spoken by many Romanies in the UK, is a language with movement at its core. It is a mixed language that has picked up influences wherever the Romanies have travelled, and so incorporates aspects of Indian, Greek, Persian, Slavic and Romance languages, creating a philological map of their wanderings north and west from, it is thought, the Indian subcontinent. In Britain and Ireland this is mixed with English and with elements from the language of Irish Travellers (known as Gamin, Shelta or Cant).

The Romani words for the months have fallen out of common use now, but records of the Welsh Romani month names exist, and these were possibly once used by Romani communities all over Britain. They show a pattern of deep connection to the land and the seasons, as well as to work and food.

The word for January, Iveskero, means 'month of the snows'. The name dates from before 'wagon time' – the time when the Romani started living in wagons – and from a period when they would travel by walking alongside their wagons, which carried the makings of simple tents. These were constructed from willow wands bent and pushed into the ground and then covered with serge, a thick woollen fabric. Snow would have meant great hardship, as well as a struggle to look after their beloved horses, which would have been covered in cloths stuffed with straw to keep the cold away.

# THE MOON

## Moon phases

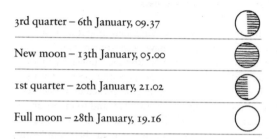

3rd quarter – 6th January, 09.37

New moon – 13th January, 05.00

1st quarter – 20th January, 21.02

Full moon – 28th January, 19.16

## Gardening by the moon

**Full moon to 3rd quarter: 1st–6th and 28th–31st.** Harvest crops for immediate eating. Harvest fruit.

**3rd quarter to new moon: 6th–13th.** Prune. Harvest for storage. Fertilise and mulch the soil.

**New moon to 1st quarter: 13th–20th.** Sow crops that develop below ground. Dig the soil.

**1st quarter to full moon: 20th–28th.** Sow crops that develop above ground. Plant seedlings and young plants.

## Moon sign – Capricorn

Astrologers believe that the new moon is a time to make plans and focus on your dreams and hopes for the period ahead, and that each new moon has a particular energy, depending on which zodiacal sign it is in. The new moon on the 13th will be in Capricorn, which is said to rule ambitions and goals, making this a good time to think about career plans and changes and how you can start to work towards them.

## Navigating by the stars, sun and moon

### Find the North Star

Sailors once had to navigate using the sun and the stars,
and it is wonderful to be able to orient yourself using them,
should you find yourself with a dark enough sky. The key
star to track down is the North Star, or Polaris. The axis of
the earth points almost exactly towards it, so in the northern
hemisphere it never sets or rises and always appears to be
sitting directly above the North Pole. In itself it is not a
particularly bright and noticeable star, but you can find it
by using a familiar asterism (cluster of stars) within Ursa
Major: the Plough, also known as the Big Dipper. Picture it as
a saucepan, and imagine a straight line running between the
two stars at the outer edge of the 'pan', Merak and Dubhe,
and extending beyond them for a distance equal to five times
their own distance apart, and you reach the North Star.

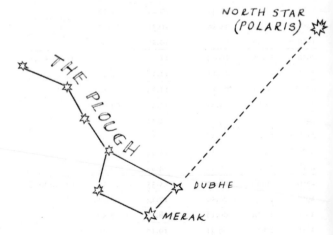

## Moon rise and set

| | St Michael's Mount | | Hopton-on-Sea | | |
|---|---|---|---|---|---|
| | Rise | Set | Rise | Set | |
| 1st | 18.54 | 10.18 | 18.13 | 10.01 | |
| 2nd | 20.10 | 10.50 | 19.31 | 10.30 | |
| 3rd | 21.28 | 11.15 | 20.52 | 10.53 | |
| 4th | 22.46 | 11.37 | 22.13 | 11.11 | |
| 5th | — | 11.56 | 23.34 | 11.28 | |
| 6th | 00.05 | 12.15 | — | 11.45 | 3rd quarter |
| 7th | 01.25 | 12.35 | 00.57 | 12.02 | |
| 8th | 02.46 | 12.58 | 02.21 | 12.22 | |
| 9th | 04.09 | 13.25 | 03.38 | 12.46 | |
| 10th | 05.32 | 14.00 | 05.13 | 13.18 | |
| 11th | 06.50 | 14.46 | 06.33 | 14.02 | |
| 12th | 07.58 | 15.45 | 07.42 | 15.00 | |
| 13th | 08.52 | 16.54 | 08.36 | 16.10 | new moon |
| 14th | 09.33 | 18.09 | 09.15 | 17.27 | |
| 15th | 10.03 | 19.25 | 09.43 | 18.46 | |
| 16th | 10.27 | 20.38 | 10.04 | 20.02 | |
| 17th | 10.47 | 21.49 | 10.22 | 21.16 | |
| 18th | 11.04 | 22.58 | 10.36 | 22.27 | |
| 19th | 11.19 | — | 10.50 | 23.36 | |
| 20th | 11.35 | 00.04 | 11.03 | — | 1st quarter |
| 21st | 11.52 | 01.11 | 11.18 | 00.45 | |
| 22nd | 12.11 | 02.18 | 11.34 | 01.54 | |
| 23rd | 12.34 | 03.25 | 11.55 | 03.04 | |
| 24th | 13.03 | 04.32 | 12.22 | 04.14 | |
| 25th | 13.40 | 05.38 | 12.57 | 05.21 | |
| 26th | 14.28 | 06.39 | 13.44 | 06.23 | |
| 27th | 15.28 | 07.32 | 14.44 | 07.16 | |
| 28th | 16.38 | 08.16 | 15.55 | 07.59 | full moon |
| 29th | 17.54 | 08.50 | 17.14 | 08.31 | |
| 30th | 19.14 | 09.18 | 18.37 | 08.57 | |
| 31st | 20.34 | 09.41 | 19.17 | 20.00 | |

Where moonset times are before moonrise times, this is the setting of
the previous night's moon.

# THE SKY

## At night

3rd and 4th: Quadrantids meteor shower. The best time for viewing will be from around 17.00 onwards on the 3rd, when the radiant will be at an altitude of 20 degrees in the northwest. Moonlight will obscure the fainter trails from around 22.00.

21st: A close approach of Mars and the moon will be visible in the dusk from around 17.00 in the southeast at an altitude of 45 degrees, until setting at 01.30 on the morning of the 22nd in the northwest.

## By day

2nd: Perihelion. This is the moment in the year at which the earth is closest to the sun in its elliptical orbit. At 13.50 the sun will be 147,093,163km away (compare with aphelion on 5th July).

21st: At solar midday the sun reaches an altitude of 19 degrees at Lee-on-the-Solent in Hampshire and 12 degrees at Lairg in Scotland.

31st: Earliest sunrise, St Michael's Mount (07.56) and Hopton-on-Sea (07.36).

31st: Latest sunset, St Michael's Mount (17.14) and Hopton-on-Sea (16.37).

1–31st: Daylight increases by 1h 8m at St Michael's Mount and by 1h 16m at Hopton-on-Sea.

## Sunrise and set

| | St Michael's Mount | | Hopton-on-Sea | |
|---|---|---|---|---|
| | Rise | Set | Rise | Set |
| 1st | 08.20 | 16.30 | 08.04 | 15.49 |
| 2nd | 08.20 | 16.31 | 08.03 | 15.50 |
| 3rd | 08.20 | 16.32 | 08.03 | 15.52 |
| 4th | 08.20 | 16.33 | 08.03 | 15.53 |
| 5th | 08.20 | 16.34 | 08.02 | 15.54 |
| 6th | 08.19 | 16.36 | 08.02 | 15.55 |
| 7th | 08.19 | 16.37 | 08.02 | 15.57 |
| 8th | 08.19 | 16.38 | 08.01 | 15.58 |
| 9th | 08.18 | 16.39 | 08.01 | 15.59 |
| 10th | 08.18 | 16.41 | 08.00 | 16.01 |
| 11th | 08.17 | 16.42 | 07.59 | 16.02 |
| 12th | 08.16 | 16.43 | 07.59 | 16.04 |
| 13th | 08.16 | 16.45 | 07.58 | 16.06 |
| 14th | 08.15 | 16.46 | 07.57 | 16.07 |
| 15th | 08.14 | 16.48 | 07.56 | 16.09 |
| 16th | 08.14 | 16.49 | 07.55 | 16.10 |
| 17th | 08.13 | 16.51 | 07.54 | 16.12 |
| 18th | 08.12 | 16.52 | 07.53 | 16.14 |
| 19th | 08.11 | 16.54 | 07.52 | 16.15 |
| 20th | 08.10 | 16.56 | 07.51 | 16.17 |
| 21st | 08.09 | 16.57 | 07.50 | 16.19 |
| 22nd | 08.08 | 16.59 | 07.48 | 16.21 |
| 23rd | 08.07 | 17.00 | 07.47 | 16.22 |
| 24th | 08.06 | 17.02 | 07.46 | 16.24 |
| 25th | 08.04 | 17.04 | 07.45 | 16.26 |
| 26th | 08.03 | 17.05 | 07.43 | 16.28 |
| 27th | 08.02 | 17.07 | 07.42 | 16.30 |
| 28th | 08.01 | 17.09 | 07.40 | 16.32 |
| 29th | 07.59 | 17.10 | 07.39 | 16.33 |
| 30th | 07.58 | 17.12 | 07.37 | 16.35 |
| 31st | 07.56 | 17.14 | 07.36 | 16.37 |

# THE SEA

**Average sea temperature**

| | |
|---|---|
| Orkney: | 7.8°C |
| South Shields: | 7.3°C |
| Carrickfergus: | 8.8°C |
| Lowestoft: | 6.8°C |
| Aberystwyth: | 8.7°C |
| Bantry: | 10.3°C |
| Cowes: | 9.6°C |
| Penzance: | 10.1°C |

**Spring and neap tides**

The spring tides are the most extreme tides of the month, with the highest rises and falls, and the neap tides are the least extreme, with the smallest. Exact timings vary around the coast, but expect them around the following dates:

**Spring tides:** 2nd–3rd and 15th–16th

**Neap tides:** 8th–9th and 23rd–24th

In the tide timetable opposite, spring tides are shown with an asterisk.

## January tide timetable for Dover

For guidance on how to convert this for your local area, see page 8.

|  | High water | | Low water | |
|---|---|---|---|---|
|  | Morning | Afternoon | Morning | Afternoon |
| 1st | 12.11 | 07.21 | 19.39 | — |
| 2nd | 00.33 | 12.49 | 08.01 | 20.17 * |
| 3rd | 01.13 | 13.30 | 08.41 | 20.56 * |
| 4th | 01.56 | 14.16 | 09.23 | 21.37 |
| 5th | 02.45 | 15.09 | 10.09 | 22.24 |
| 6th | 03.41 | 16.11 | 11.01 | 23.20 |
| 7th | 04.46 | 17.27 | — | 12.03 |
| 8th | 05.59 | 18.47 | 00.29 | 13.11 |
| 9th | 07.13 | 19.56 | 01.41 | 14.19 |
| 10th | 08.20 | 20.57 | 02.51 | 15.28 |
| 11th | 09.20 | 21.52 | 04.01 | 16.39 |
| 12th | 10.16 | 22.42 | 05.08 | 17.43 |
| 13th | 11.05 | 23.26 | 06.06 | 18.37 |
| 14th | 11.50 | — | 06.58 | 19.24 |
| 15th | 00.08 | 12.32 | 07.44 | 20.05 * |
| 16th | 00.50 | 13.13 | 08.27 | 20.42 * |
| 17th | 01.30 | 13.53 | 09.05 | 21.15 |
| 18th | 02.11 | 14.34 | 09.39 | 21.43 |
| 19th | 02.51 | 15.17 | 10.10 | 22.11 |
| 20th | 03.32 | 16.05 | 10.43 | 22.47 |
| 21st | 04.20 | 17.02 | 11.25 | 23.36 |
| 22nd | 05.18 | 18.09 | — | 12.24 |
| 23rd | 06.27 | 19.16 | 00.48 | 13.35 |
| 24th | 07.34 | 20.16 | 02.07 | 14.42 |
| 25th | 08.31 | 21.06 | 03.13 | 15.41 |
| 26th | 09.20 | 21.50 | 04.09 | 16.33 |
| 27th | 10.03 | 22.29 | 04.58 | 17.21 |
| 28th | 10.43 | 23.06 | 05.44 | 18.07 |
| 29th | 11.22 | 23.44 | 06.28 | 18.50 |
| 30th | — | 12.00 | 07.12 | 19.32 |
| 31st | 00.21 | 12.39 | 07.55 | 20.12 |

# A SEA SHANTY FOR JANUARY

## Hieland Laddie

For hundreds of years whaling was a huge part of the Scottish economy, with men setting off in whaleboats from the Scottish east-coast ports of Dundee and Peterhead to catch bowhead whales off Greenland in unimaginably cold, harsh and dangerous conditions. Happily, ever since the hunting of blue and humpback whales was banned globally in 1966 and a moratorium on commercial whaling took effect in 1986, the population has recovered significantly.

Shanties were working songs, from a time when human muscle had to do what steam and oil did later. The shanties kept men working together in time as they hauled and heaved on the various ropes and pumps on a merchant sailing vessel. Each shanty had a different use. This is a 'walkaway' shanty for a continual hauling action, requiring a line of men to hold a rope and walk backwards while hauling on it. They would run back to the start of the line when they ran out of space. Such shanties generally had long choruses suited to the action.

Where have ye been when I looked for ye,
Heiland laddie, bonnie laddie?
Where have ye been when I looked for ye,
Me bonnie Hieland laddie O?
*Way, hay an' away we go,*
*Hieland laddie! Bonnie laddie!*
*Way, hay an' away we go,*
*Me bonnie Hieland laddie O!*

Joined a ship and went a-sailin'
Heiland laddie! Bonnie laddie!
Sailed far north and went a-whalin'
Me bonnie Hieland laddie O!
*Way, hay...*

Bound away to Iceland cold
Heiland laddie! Bonnie laddie!
Found much ice but not much gold
Me bonnie Hieland laddie O!
*Way, hay...*

I'll be glad when I get hame
Heiland laddie! Bonnie laddie!
I'll give up this whalin' game
Me bonnie Hieland laddie O!
*Way, hay...*

Soon be homeward bound to Scotland
Heiland laddie! Bonnie laddie!
Homeward bound to bonnie Scotland
Me bonnie Hieland laddie O!
*Way, hay...*

SVALBARD

FIRTH of FORTH

CARIBBEAN

A MAP OF HUMPBACK WHALE MIGRATION

# MIGRATION OF THE MONTH

### Humpback whale migration

Humpback whales everywhere are epic travellers, journeying back and forth between high-latitude areas of the world (the Arctic or Antarctic Circle) and the equator, making full luxuriant use of all of the water temperatures the world has to offer, according to the season and their needs. There are populations in every ocean, and those of the Atlantic trek over 5,000km from the icy seas north of the Arctic Circle off Norway in summer, teeming with herring, mackerel and krill, down to the warm lapping waters of the Caribbean in late winter. They feed themselves up in the north, and give birth to and rear their young in the south. And on their way they pass us, this month.

Their migration is usually pelagic, which means that they move through the open sea, well away from land. But one group, having summered in the feeding grounds off the Norwegian islands of Svalbard, have started making a Scottish stop-off in the Firth of Forth, presumably to refuel and set them up for the onward journey. Since 2017 – and despite very few humpback whale sightings in the Firth of Forth before then – there have been increasing numbers of sightings each year. This dramatic change ties in with a slow but steady recovery in the population of Atlantic humpback whales since the demise of whaling, which was a major industry in Scotland for hundreds of years. It is thought that as the whale population has increased, whales have started returning to areas they had previously been driven out of, and perhaps this is happening here.

They will not stay for long and will be on their way again before the end of the month, having made full use of our krill and delighted our whale watchers. Once they reach the Caribbean, the females will give birth to live young, nudging them up to the surface to take their first breath, and they will stay with them and nurse them for the whole of their first year.

# THE GARDEN

### January garden meditation

In January it is so tempting to stay indoors and only experience the garden through a window. Take five minutes to step outside and just observe your garden, or do the same in a park if you don't have a garden of your own. You may initially see just mess and mud but the purpose of this exercise all year long is going to be to look for the beauty in the outdoors during every moment in the year.

So what do you see, hear and feel? Consider taking your shoes and socks off and then stand barefoot on the cold earth and think: what is good about this moment? Perhaps the light is beautiful. Perhaps it is quiet. Maybe your body is warm from a good, thick coat while the soles of your feet are tingling and alive with cold. Think about the moment you will go back inside and warm them up. Describe the colour of the sky to yourself: piercing blue or dappled with cloud? If the sun is on your face or back, think about how it warms you from nearly 150 million kilometres away. Think about how its strength will increase as the year goes on and how that will feel.

And look for signs. Even now, in these dark and cold days, bulbs are starting to push their little green spears up through the earth. If you can't see anything yet, think about all that life held suspended.

## Jobs in the garden

- This is planning time: what do you want to grow this year? Make lists and start ordering seeds.
- Don't begin clearing old, dead growth yet – all sorts of creatures could be hunkering down in there.
- Plant a fruit tree. Choose carefully and consider seeking out a heritage variety suited to your area. It will be with you for a long time.

## How much to sow

It is tempting to sow whole packets of seeds and then be overwhelmed by seedlings or, later, great gluts of one type of vegetable. This guide will help you to sow roughly the amount you need for a family of four; adjust to suit your own circumstances and favourites. In every case, sow a small number more than suggested to allow for non-germination and seedling failure. There is not a huge amount of seed sowing to be done this month, but there are a few things you can start off.

**Chillies:** Unless you are an absolute chilli fiend, one plant each of two or three different varieties should do.

**Peas:** You will want a thickly sown row around a metre long, but at the moment sow them into pots to be planted out later – perhaps half a big packet.

**Broad beans:** You need a lot of broad bean plants to end up with a decent number of beans on your plate. If you already sowed a row in autumn, sow another 15 seeds now indoors, in long pots like root trainers; this should be enough to make a 3-m row of plants planted 23cm apart. If you didn't (and you have planting out space), double this number.

# THE KITCHEN

### Romani recipe for January – Rasher pudding

Bacon features in many Romani recipes as it is easy to store and carry, and puddings like this were good for filling stomachs on cold days and making a little meat go a long way. Recipe by Julie Jones, née Ayres, via her grandson Damian Le Bas. Julie was born in a Reading wagon at Shaldon Green in Hampshire on 27th January 1927, when the snow lay in deep drifts all around. Reading wagons are a type of Romani wagon named after their original builder, Dunton and Sons of Reading.

Mix 2 handfuls of suet with about 450g plain flour and enough water to make a dough. On a floured surface, roll the dough out flat into a roughly square shape. Lay 12 rashers of streaky bacon evenly across it. Cut an onion into thin slices and sprinkle across the rashers, then add a little pepper. Roll the whole thing up so it looks like a jam roly-poly, then squidge the ends together to seal them (so it ends up looking more like a sausage). Tie it up with a clean muslin or tea towel, using string to tie the ends. Boil in a large pan for a couple of hours, drain for several minutes and then slice thickly. Serve immediately, sprinkled with salt and vinegar if you like. Leftovers can be sliced and carried out as a cold snack, or sliced and fried.

## In season

### In the hedgerows, woods and fields
**Wild greens:** Chickweed, hairy bittercress, dandelion leaves, sow thistle, wintercress
**Game:** Pheasant, goose, partridge, rabbit, snipe, mallard, woodcock, venison

### From the seashore and rivers
**Fish and shellfish:** Mussels, oysters, scallops, turbot, cod, whiting, Dover sole, haddock, pollock, bass

### From the kitchen garden
**Vegetables:** Purple sprouting broccoli, carrots, Brussels sprouts, turnips, beetroot, spinach, Jerusalem artichoke, kale, chard, lettuce, chicory, endive, cauliflower, cabbages, celeriac, swede, leeks, forced rhubarb
**Herbs:** Winter savory, parsley, chervil, coriander, rosemary, bay, sage

### From the farms
Stilton

### And traditional imports
Seville oranges, bergamot oranges, truffles

# RECIPES

### Caramelised pear Galette des Rois

There are various versions of Galette des Rois, or 'king cake', to celebrate the arrival of the Three Kings to Bethlehem at Epiphany. This is the French version, and perhaps the best known: the galette of kings, a pithivier of flaky puff pastry and almond frangipane. In this version there is also a layer of caramelised pear sandwiched into the gooey centre. Tradition has it that the cake contains a *fève*, once a broad bean, now more usually a tiny figurine representing the king, and that the cake is topped by a gold paper crown. The person whose piece contains the *fève* wears the crown and becomes king or queen for the night.

| Serves 8 |
| --- |
| **Ingredients** |
| 150g butter, softened |
| 2 unripe pears, peeled, cored and sliced |
| 150g golden caster sugar |
| Seeds of 1 vanilla pod |
| 2 eggs, lightly beaten |
| 100g ground almonds |
| 2 tablespoons cognac |
| 400g all butter puff pastry |

**Method**
Preheat the oven to 200°C/Gas Mark 6. Start by cooking the pear. Melt 50g of the butter in a wide-bottomed pan, add the pear slices and fry until they start to caramelise. Add 50g of the sugar and the vanilla and continue cooking until the sugar has dissolved completely and has glazed and further caramelised the pear pieces. Spoon onto a plate, pour over any juices, and leave to cool.

Beat the remaining butter and sugar together until light and fluffy, and then mix in half of the beaten egg until it is incorporated well. Add the ground almonds and cognac, and mix.

Divide the pastry into 2 pieces and roll each out on a floured surface to make 2 rounds, each 25cm in diameter. Place a pastry round on parchment on a baking sheet. Spread the almond mixture evenly over it, and then the pear mixture, leaving behind any excess liquid. Paint the edge with a little of the remaining beaten egg and then place the second round over the top. Press down the edges to seal, and cut a toothed edge. Paint all over with the rest of the beaten egg and then use the tip of a sharp knife to cut a pattern in the top. Usually this is a series of semicircles emanating from a centre point, but be creative. Bake for 25–30 minutes, or until the top is golden brown and the pastry risen and crispy. Serve warm with double cream.

### Lambswool with apple brandy

This was a traditional medieval drink for Twelfth Night or Epiphany and was also used to bless the apple trees in traditional wassailing ceremonies held around this date. The name refers to the fluff of cooked apple that rises to the top of the mulled cider or ale. Be sure to use Bramley apples, or you won't get the fluff.

---

**Serves 8–10**

---

**Ingredients**

---

6 Bramley apples

---

1.5 litres cider or real ale

---

150g brown sugar

---

Half a nutmeg, grated

---

2.5cm piece ginger root, peeled and finely grated

---

Apple brandy (optional)

---

**Method**

Preheat the oven to 190°c/Gas Mark 5. Core the apples and place them in a baking dish, covered with foil. Bake for 30–45 minutes, or until very soft and collapsing, then remove and leave to cool a little. Put the cider or ale into a saucepan with the sugar, nutmeg and ginger, and heat gently to dissolve the sugar. Scoop the apples out of their skins and mash with a fork, then add them to the pot. Cook gently for 10–15 minutes. Give the mixture a quick blast with a hand-held blender, to further break up the apple. Serve hot in heatproof glasses or mugs and top with a shot of apple brandy, if desired.

# PILGRIMAGE OF THE MONTH

## Epiphany/Blessing of the Waters, Margate

The word epiphany means a moment of clarity, a sudden revelation of deep understanding. The Christian festival of Epiphany celebrates two moments of epiphany within Jesus' life. The Western church marks 6th January as the moment when the Magi completed their epic pilgrimage to pay homage to the newborn king. While the shepherds were there at the birth, the Magi followed the Star of Bethlehem and arrived many months, possibly up to two years, later. The only information given in the Bible on the route of this first Christian pilgrimage is that they came 'from the rising [of the sun]' and it seems likely that they travelled along the Silk Road that ran from Asia through Persia and into Arabia. Their arrival at Jesus' home in Bethlehem was the 'manifestation of Christ to the Gentiles' (gentiles being non-Jews): the first revelation to outsiders that he was something special, hence 'epiphany'.

In the Eastern Orthodox Christian tradition, Epiphany celebrates the baptism of Christ at around 30 years of age. Jesus was baptised by St John the Baptist in the River Jordan, and this was his manifestation to the world as the son of God, and so humanity's epiphany. Orthodox Epiphany falls on 19th January as Orthodox churches still follow the Julian calendar.

Orthodox churches mark the day with a 'Blessing of the Waters' – a sort of mini-pilgrimage. On the evening before Epiphany, the Great Blessing of the Waters is carried out inside church at the baptismal font. The next day the congregation make a Crucession (a procession with a cross) from the church to the nearest body of water, where a dove is released. The priest blesses the waters then throws the cross into the water, and hardy young people leap in to find it. The one to return the cross to the priest is given a special blessing for the year ahead. The British Greek Orthodox community gathers in Margate, Kent, each January for a Blessing of the Seas procession led by the Archbishop of Thyateira and Great Britain.

# February

 St Brigid's Day (Christian)

 Start of LGBT+ history month

 1st–2nd: Imbolc (Gaelic/pagan/neopagan celebration)

 Candlemas (Christian)

 Chinese New Year – Year of the Ox begins

 St Valentine's Day/Birds' Wedding Day

 Parinirvana Day/Nirvana Day – celebrating Buddha's life and achievement of parinirvana (Buddhist)

Vasant Panchami (Hindu spring festival)

Shrove Tuesday – pancake day (Christian/tradition)

Ash Wednesday – start of Lent (Christian)

25th–26th: Purim (Jewish celebration)

# ROMANI NAME FOR THE MONTH

## Bita kaulo munthos – little black month

This name must be a reference to the fact that this is the last of the dark months of winter, when the daylight hours are very short. An alternative Romani name for February is Kaulay Staur Kurkay, which means 'dark four weeks'. As the Romani would have been living in tents at the time that these names were widely used, daylight hours would have been very precious, and the gloom and cold of a short February day would have been hard to bear. Then, as now, Romani families would most likely have stopped for the winter at a place that they returned to every year – one of the *atchin tans*, the stopping places that once peppered Britain and Ireland but are now rare. This month, however, they may well have set off on the road and camped next to snowdrop woods, where the women and children would pick wild snowdrops, gather them into posies and sell them door to door, returning to make a stew cooked on an outdoor fire each evening, perhaps eaten with a handful of the first young leaves of wild garlic.

The root *kaul*, meaning 'black', comes up again and again in their language for words meaning 'Romani', including *kaulesko* ('of a Romani man') and *kauliako* ('of a Romani woman), presumably referring to the dark skin and hair the Romani sometimes have, a pointer to their probable Indian ancestry. Other related words take it on, too, including *kaulengay patrinyau*, meaning 'Gypsy trail'. Already in February the Romanies would be back on the trail that took them around the harvests and through the seasons of wild flowers, crops, crafting and gatherings. The travelling year had begun.

# THE MOON

## Moon phases

3rd quarter – 4th February, 17.37

New moon – 11th February, 19.06

1st quarter – 19th February, 18.47

Full moon – 27th February, 08.17

## Gardening by the moon

**Full moon to 3rd quarter: 1st–4th and 27th–28th.** Harvest crops for immediate eating. Harvest fruit.

**3rd quarter to new moon: 4th–11th.** Prune. Harvest for storage. Fertilise and mulch the soil.

**New moon to 1st quarter: 11th–19th.** Sow crops that develop below ground. Dig the soil.

**1st quarter to full moon: 19th–27th.** Sow crops that develop above ground. Plant seedlings and young plants.

## Moon sign – Aquarius

Astrologers believe that the new moon is a time to make plans and focus on your dreams and hopes for the period ahead, and that each new moon has a particular energy, depending on which zodiacal sign it is in. The new moon on the 11th will be in Aquarius, which is said to be an unconventional and trailblazing sign, making this a good time to give your most inventive thoughts and ideas space to breathe.

**Navigating by the stars, sun and moon**

**Find your latitude using the North Star**
Once you have located the North Star (see page 14), you can
use it to discover your latitude – that is, how many degrees
above the equator is the spot where you are standing. Latitude
is 0 degrees at the equator and 90 degrees at the North Pole,
so if you are in the northern hemisphere you are somewhere
between the two. Facing the North Star, stretch your arms out
straight ahead of you and form your hands into fists. Now
place one fist on top of the other, counting as you go, until you
reach the star. Each fist counts as roughly 10 degrees, and added
together will give you your latitude. Alternatively, you can use
your outstretched hand, which will equal around 20 degrees.
So if you are standing near the equator, the North Star will be
close to the horizon and you will get a reading of 0 degrees or
thereabouts, whereas if you are in the Arctic Circle, it will be
high in the sky and your reading will be close to 90 degrees.

NORTH STAR

10°

10°

## Moon rise and set

| | St Michael's Mount | | Hopton-on-Sea | | |
|---|---|---|---|---|---|
| | Rise | Set | Rise | Set | |
| 1st | 21.54 | 10.02 | 21.22 | 09.35 | |
| 2nd | 23.14 | 10.21 | 22.46 | 09.51 | |
| 3rd | — | 10.40 | — | 10.08 | |
| 4th | 00.35 | 11.02 | 00.09 | 10.27 | 3rd quarter |
| 5th | 01.57 | 11.27 | 01.34 | 10.49 | |
| 6th | 03.18 | 11.59 | 02.58 | 11.18 | |
| 7th | 04.36 | 12.39 | 04.19 | 11.56 | |
| 8th | 05.45 | 13.32 | 05.30 | 12.47 | |
| 9th | 06.43 | 14.36 | 06.28 | 13.51 | |
| 10th | 07.28 | 15.48 | 07.11 | 15.05 | |
| 11th | 08.02 | 17.03 | 07.43 | 16.23 | new moon |
| 12th | 08.28 | 18.18 | 08.07 | 17.41 | |
| 13th | 08.50 | 19.30 | 08.25 | 18.56 | |
| 14th | 09.07 | 20.41 | 08.41 | 20.09 | |
| 15th | 09.24 | 21.49 | 08.55 | 21.19 | |
| 16th | 09.39 | 22.56 | 09.08 | 22.29 | |
| 17th | 09.55 | — | 09.22 | 23.38 | |
| 18th | 10.13 | 00.03 | 09.38 | — | |
| 19th | 10.34 | 01.10 | 09.56 | 00.48 | 1st quarter |
| 20th | 11.00 | 02.17 | 10.20 | 01.58 | |
| 21st | 11.33 | 03.23 | 10.51 | 03.06 | |
| 22nd | 12.16 | 04.26 | 11.32 | 04.10 | |
| 23rd | 13.10 | 05.22 | 12.25 | 05.07 | |
| 24th | 14.16 | 06.09 | 13.32 | 05.53 | |
| 25th | 15.30 | 06.47 | 14.49 | 06.29 | |
| 26th | 16.50 | 07.18 | 16.11 | 06.58 | |
| 27th | 18.12 | 07.43 | 17.36 | 07.20 | full moon |
| 28th | 19.34 | 08.05 | 19.02 | 07.39 | |

Where moonset times are before moonrise times, this is the setting of
the previous night's moon.

# THE SKY

## At night

**18th:** Close approach of Mars and the moon, visible in the dusk from around 17.30 in the south at an altitude of 55 degrees, until setting at 00.30 on the 19th in the northwest.

## By day

**21st:** At solar midday the sun reaches an altitude of 22 degrees at Lee-on-the-Solent in Hampshire and 12 degrees at Lairg in Scotland.

**28th:** Earliest sunrise, St Michael's Mount (07.07) and Hopton-on-Sea (06.41).

**28th:** Latest sunset, St Michael's Mount (18.02) and Hopton-on-Sea (17.30).

**1st–28th:** Daylight increases by 1h 35m at St Michael's Mount and by 1h 45m at Hopton-on-Sea.

**Sunrise and set**

F

| | St Michael's Mount | | Hopton-on-Sea | |
|---|---|---|---|---|
| | Rise | Set | Rise | Set |
| 1st | 07.55 | 17.16 | 07.34 | 16.39 |
| 2nd | 07.54 | 17.17 | 07.32 | 16.41 |
| 3rd | 07.52 | 17.19 | 07.31 | 16.43 |
| 4th | 07.51 | 17.21 | 07.29 | 16.45 |
| 5th | 07.49 | 17.22 | 07.27 | 16.47 |
| 6th | 07.47 | 17.24 | 07.26 | 16.49 |
| 7th | 07.46 | 17.26 | 07.24 | 16.50 |
| 8th | 07.44 | 17.28 | 07.22 | 16.52 |
| 9th | 07.42 | 17.29 | 07.20 | 16.54 |
| 10th | 07.41 | 17.31 | 07.18 | 16.56 |
| 11th | 07.39 | 17.33 | 07.16 | 16.58 |
| 12th | 07.37 | 17.35 | 07.15 | 17.00 |
| 13th | 07.36 | 17.36 | 07.13 | 17.02 |
| 14th | 07.34 | 17.38 | 07.11 | 17.04 |
| 15th | 07.32 | 17.40 | 07.09 | 17.06 |
| 16th | 07.30 | 17.42 | 07.07 | 17.08 |
| 17th | 07.28 | 17.43 | 07.05 | 17.09 |
| 18th | 07.26 | 17.45 | 07.03 | 17.11 |
| 19th | 07.24 | 17.47 | 07.00 | 17.13 |
| 20th | 07.23 | 17.48 | 06.58 | 17.15 |
| 21st | 07.21 | 17.50 | 06.56 | 17.17 |
| 22nd | 07.19 | 17.52 | 06.54 | 17.19 |
| 23rd | 07.17 | 17.54 | 06.52 | 17.21 |
| 24th | 07.15 | 17.55 | 06.50 | 17.23 |
| 25th | 07.13 | 17.57 | 06.48 | 17.25 |
| 26th | 07.11 | 17.59 | 06.45 | 17.26 |
| 27th | 07.09 | 18.00 | 06.43 | 17.28 |
| 28th | 07.07 | 18.02 | 06.41 | 17.30 |

# THE SEA

## Average sea temperature

| | |
|---|---|
| Orkney: | 7.3°C |
| South Shields: | 6.8°C |
| Carrickfergus: | 8.1°C |
| Lowestoft: | 6.5°C |
| Aberystwyth: | 8.3°C |
| Bantry: | 10.2°C |
| Cowes: | 9.1°C |
| Penzance: | 9.7°C |

## Spring and neap tides

The spring tides are the most extreme tides of the month, with the highest rises and falls, and the neap tides are the least extreme, with the smallest. Exact timings vary around the coast, but expect them around the following dates:

**Spring tides:** 1st–2nd and 14th–15th

**Neap tides:** 7th–8th and 21st–22nd

In the tide timetable opposite, spring tides are shown with an asterisk.

## February tide timetable for Dover

For guidance on how to convert this for your local area, see page 8.

|  | *High water* | | *Low water* | |
|---|---|---|---|---|
|  | Morning | Afternoon | Morning | Afternoon |
| 1st | 01.01 | 13.18 | 08.36 | 20.49 * |
| 2nd | 01.42 | 14.00 | 09.15 | 21.27 * |
| 3rd | 02.27 | 14.47 | 09.55 | 22.07 |
| 4th | 03.15 | 15.40 | 10.39 | 22.55 |
| 5th | 04.12 | 16.45 | 11.32 | 23.54 |
| 6th | 05.21 | 18.11 | — | 12.37 |
| 7th | 06.47 | 19.37 | 01.08 | 13.51 |
| 8th | 08.12 | 20.50 | 02.26 | 15.09 |
| 9th | 09.23 | 21.50 | 03.48 | 16.36 |
| 10th | 10.21 | 22.38 | 05.06 | 17.43 |
| 11th | 11.07 | 23.19 | 06.05 | 18.34 |
| 12th | 11.46 | 23.57 | 06.54 | 19.17 |
| 13th | — | 12.21 | 07.36 | 19.53 |
| 14th | 00.34 | 12.55 | 08.12 | 20.22 * |
| 15th | 01.10 | 13.29 | 08.42 | 20.47 * |
| 16th | 01.44 | 14.01 | 09.07 | 21.07 |
| 17th | 02.14 | 14.31 | 09.28 | 21.31 |
| 18th | 02.40 | 15.01 | 09.54 | 22.02 |
| 19th | 03.11 | 15.37 | 10.28 | 22.41 |
| 20th | 03.56 | 16.48 | 11.13 | 23.35 |
| 21st | 05.18 | 18.26 | — | 12.26 |
| 22nd | 06.50 | 19.37 | 01.07 | 13.59 |
| 23rd | 07.59 | 20.37 | 02.34 | 15.10 |
| 24th | 08.55 | 21.25 | 03.39 | 16.08 |
| 25th | 09.42 | 22.07 | 04.34 | 17.01 |
| 26th | 10.25 | 22.46 | 05.24 | 17.50 |
| 27th | 11.04 | 23.25 | 06.12 | 18.36 |
| 28th | 11.43 | — | 06.59 | 19.19 |

# A SEA SHANTY FOR FEBRUARY

### Hooraw for the Black Ball Line

A song for the 'little black month', and for the snow and ice that often come with it. The Black Ball Line was a series of packet ships that ran between Liverpool and New York from 1816 until around 1850, keeping a pretty much regular timetable from 1822 with two sailings per month in all weathers. It was the first line of sailing ships to take passengers and carried many hopeful migrants to the New World to seek their fortunes in the gold mines. It was named after its flag, a black ball on a red background.

This is a 'capstan' shanty. Heavy jobs such as raising the anchor used a capstan, a sort of vertical barrel with spokes that the sailors walked around, one pushing on each spoke, which would gradually pull in the anchor or other rope. These jobs being particularly lengthy and laborious, many capstan shanties have long verses and grand choruses, for joining in, though this one in particular doesn't follow that pattern.

In the Black-ball Line I served my time, To me way, oh hay, hoo-raw! In the Black-ball Line I served my time, Hoo-raw for the Black-ball Line!

Blackball ships are good and true,
*To me way, oh hay, hooraw!*
They are the ships for me and you,
*Hooraw for the Blackball Line!*

I've sailed that line full many a time
*To me way...*
It's there I wasted all me prime
*Hooraw...*

Just take a ship to Liverpool
*To me way...*
To Liverpool that packet school
*Hooraw...*

Yankee sailors you'll see there
*To me way...*
With red-topped boots and short-cut hair
*Hooraw...*

The ship will go through ice an' snow
*To me way...*
And take ye where the winds don't blow
*Hooraw...*

Oh, drink a health to the Blackball Line
*To me way...*
Their ships are stout, their men are fine
*Hooraw...*

# THE GARDEN

### February garden meditation

February is another tough month in which to find the good things, but if there are any, they'll be in the garden. Step outside, remove your shoes and socks if you are feeling brave, and feel the cold earth coming up through the soles of your feet. This can be a grey and gloomy old month, but even if it is, what sort of grey? Is it a solid, heavy, gunmetal grey, or a shining and pewter shade? A mottled horse's flank or a thunderous, billowing menace? Find precise words for what you see. Breathe in the cold air and feel it fill your lungs. Notice the sting of cold rain against your skin, feeling how alive you are. And listen. Maybe you will just hear the rumbling of traffic but you might detect a blackbird singing its heart out. Think about how life is stirring all around you and beneath you, unseen, triggered by the incremental change in light levels and warmth. There are visible signs of it, too: rhubarb pushing up from the soil, pure and perfect dangling snowdrops, constellations of winter aconites, shiny frog and toad spawn in the pond.

## Jobs in the garden

- Rake over your seedbeds and weed them to get them ready for direct sowing. You might cover them with cloches or clear plastic to help them warm up and be a more receptive place for your seeds.
- Plant roses, either bare root or potted, though bare-root roses are cheaper if you can find them. Prune the bush roses you already have by cutting them back by about a third, to an outward-facing bud.
- Get hold of some coppiced hazel twigs and use them to make supports for your perennials and roses once they start growing. Bend them into domes and push the ends into the earth and then weave other stems all around them.

## How much to sow

It is tempting to sow whole packets of seeds and then be overwhelmed by seedlings or, later, great gluts of one type of vegetable. This guide will help you to sow roughly the amount you need for a family of four; adjust to suit your own circumstances and favourites. In every case, sow a small number more than suggested to allow for non-germination and seedling failure.

**Aubergines and sweet peppers:** Under cover in a heated propagator, sow six plants of three different cultivars of each.
**Sprouting broccoli:** Under cover in pots, sow four plants of two different varieties.

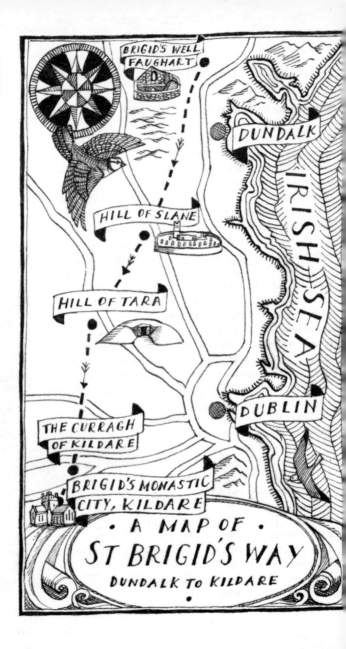

BRIGID'S WELL
FAUGHART

DUNDALK

IRISH SEA

HILL OF SLANE

HILL OF TARA

DUBLIN

THE CURRAGH
OF KILDARE

BRIGID'S MONASTIC
CITY, KILDARE

• A MAP OF •
St BRIGID'S WAY
DUNDALK TO KILDARE

# PILGRIMAGE OF THE MONTH

## Brigid's Way for St Brigid's Day

The first day of February is St Brigid's Day, a day of two women: one goddess and one saint, one from Ireland's pagan past and one from its Christian past. The goddess Brigid was one of the Tuatha Dé Danann, Ireland's mythical ancient race of gods. She was a healer, a poet and a smith, and is associated with spring, wells and fertility. She is also strongly associated with Imbolc, the Gaelic festival marking the end of winter and the beginning of early spring, which falls on 1st February. Imbolc means 'in the belly' and falls as lambing begins.

Brigid's Christian counterpart, St Brigid of Kildare, who was born in the fifth century and shares many of the same attributes, is one of the three patron saints of Ireland, along with Patrick and Columba. Her own feast day falls on the same day as Imbolc. Have their identities merged over the centuries or were they always – as some would have it – one and the same? It has been argued that Christian monks may have taken the goddess's attributes and grafted on the name of the saint in order to make use of the cult of Brigid in spreading the new religion through Ireland.

Either way, many people are now ready to turn back and embrace both aspects of Brigid, and this has led to the creation of a new pilgrimage based on ancient pilgrim paths and wells, Brigid's Way. It begins at St Brigid's birthplace at Faughart, in Co. Louth, and finishes in Kildare town, where Brigid founded a monastery. The 146-km route takes in holy wells dedicated to Brigid, as well as the Cuchulainn Stone, the Hill of Slane, the Hill of Tara and Brigid's Fire Temple, where nuns kept a flame burning until the suppression of the monasteries in the 16th century (and where the tradition was resurrected by the Brigidine Sisters in 1993). The ancient sites form a cross in the landscape, echoing the shape of St Brigid's Cross, an offset cross that is woven from rushes and placed over doorways and windows to protect against harm.

# THE KITCHEN

### Romani recipe for February – Rhubarb drink

This is a simple drink made through the year from whatever fruit was to hand, which in February would be rhubarb. Recipe based on the research of Romani and Traveller historian Robert Dawson.

Make a rhubarb drink by dissolving 350ml sugar in 300ml hot water. Add 600ml of the juice of stewed and sieved rhubarb. Chill before serving. Make this with blackberries in the summer.

### In season

### In the hedgerows, woods and fields
**Wild greens:** Chickweed, hairy bittercress, dandelion leaves, sow thistle, wintercress
**Roots:** Wild garlic
**Game:** Rabbit, hare, mallard, partridge, pheasant, venison

### From the seashore and rivers
**Fish and shellfish:** Mussels, oysters, scallops, turbot, cockles, mussels, lemon sole, bass, bream, cod, whiting, haddock

### From the kitchen garden
**Vegetables:** Purple sprouting broccoli, carrots, Brussels sprouts, turnips, beetroots, spinach, Jerusalem artichoke, kale, chard, lettuce, chicory and endive, cauliflower, cabbages, celeriac, swede, leeks, turnips, forced rhubarb
**Herbs:** Winter savory, parsley, chervil, coriander, rosemary, bay, sage

### From the farms
Stilton

### And traditional imports
Seville oranges, blood oranges

# RECIPES

### Wild garlic boxty

St Brigid, whose feast day falls at the beginning of the month, is the patron saint of several delicious things, including dairy, and is also linked to marriage and fertility. Boxty is traditionally eaten on the day, and this may be because of the lashings of buttermilk and butter involved in its making, but could equally be because it is considered an essential component of matrimony as evidenced by the traditional rhyme: 'Boxty on the griddle, boxty in the pan, if you can't make boxty, you'll never get a man.' Young wild garlic is up in the woods this month, and if you can get hold of some it makes a very delicious addition.

| Makes about 12 |
| --- |
| **Ingredients** |
| 225g hot boiled potatoes |
| 225g grated raw potato |
| 300g plain flour |
| 1 teaspoon bicarbonate of soda |
| Handful of wild garlic leaves, washed and torn up |
| About 350ml buttermilk (or full fat milk with the juice of half a lemon added then left for a few minutes) |
| Butter for frying |
| Salt and pepper |

### Method
Mash the hot potatoes and mix with the raw potato. Add the flour, bicarbonate of soda, wild garlic and salt and pepper. Mix, then add enough of the buttermilk to form it into a pliable dough. Form into flat rounds 7.5cm wide and 1.5cm thick, and fry in butter until golden on each side. To get

the right texture it is important that you make them ahead of time, rest them, and then refry them just before eating, perhaps with a poached egg and a piece of bacon (bacon is also happily presided over by St Brigid).


### Seville orange syllabub

Another recipe to mark St Brigid's Day, patron saint of dairy, or just to celebrate the arrival of the Seville oranges if you can spare one from your marmalade making. It's very simple and quick to make, but you do need to start this the day before you are going to eat it.

| Serves 6–8 |
| --- |
| **Ingredients** |
| 50g caster sugar |
| Grated zest of 1 Seville orange |
| 3 tablespoons Seville orange juice |
| 100ml Madeira or brandy |
| 300ml double cream |

**Method**
Put the sugar, zest, juice and alcohol into a bowl and leave to steep overnight. The next day add the cream and start to whisk with an electric beater or by hand. Stop when you feel it begin to thicken, and tip it into little glasses, then refrigerate until needed. You could serve with digestive biscuits to crumble on top.

# MIGRATION OF THE MONTH

## Toad migration

This month's migration is perhaps not the most epic of our journeys, and the mode of travel is hardly the most elegant, but it is happening almost under our feet, and is as perilous and fraught with danger as any globetrotting trek. Throughout this month, toads will start to stir, having been firmly tucked away until now in their winter hibernacula (where they hibernate) in the mud at the bottom of ponds, under piles of leaves or dug deep down in the ground below the frost line.

Although they have evolved the ability to live their entire lives on dry land, toads still must have water to breed. By the end of the month they will be on the move, the males setting out first, plodding rather than hopping towards the ponds where they were born. They have incredible homing instincts and will travel for several miles, moving at night to avoid the sun, steadfastly making their way over every obstacle. Or at least attempting to. There is clearly great danger in crossing roads at toad's pace at night, and every year there are a large number of casualties, sometimes mitigated by 'toad patrols'. (Look for one to join locally and help to usher toads safely through the night.) If you see 'toads crossing' signs when driving, slow right down to toad-dodging speed. Intensive agriculture and the loss of many dew ponds have had a big impact on toad populations, but garden ponds have come to the rescue – as often as not it is now these ponds that toads migrate towards in this great annual amphibian ramble.

The only thing that eases the male toad's tricky passage is if he chances upon a female toad, in which case he won't hesitate to climb upon her back and piggyback a lift the rest of the way. Once home pond is reached, the coupled-up pair will breed – or if a female arrives alone, then a load of males will jump on her to form a 'toad ball', all trying their luck. Long strings of eggs encased in jelly are laid right across the pond. After 14 days the jelly disintegrates and the tadpoles drop into the water to begin life in their own home pond.

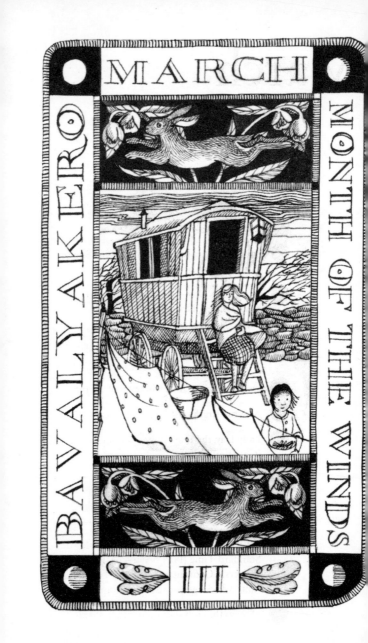

# March

 Start of meteorological spring

 St David's Day – patron saint of Wales

 St Piran's Day – patron saint of Cornwall

 Commonwealth Day

 Fourth Sunday in Lent – Mothering Sunday (Christian/traditional)

 St Patrick's Day – patron saint of Ireland – bank holiday, Northern Ireland and Republic of Ireland

 Vernal equinox – start of astronomical spring

 Ostara (neopagan celebration of spring)

 Nowruz (Iranian/Persian New Year)

 Lady Day, the Feast of the Annunciation (Christian)

 Palm Sunday (Christian)

 First day of Passover/Pesach (Jewish) – festivities begin the evening before

 British Summer Time (BST) and Irish Standard Time (IST) begin – both are Universal Coordinated Time (UTC) + 1 hour. Clocks go forward one hour at 01.00

 28th–29th: Holi (Hindu spring festival)

# ROMANI NAME FOR THE MONTH

## Bavalyakero – month of the winds

March is blustery and blowy, the cheery daffodils are battered (they don't seem to mind) and the tree branches with their new buds are being swished to and fro. This is because March is one of the transition months. With days growing longer and the sun higher in the sky, we are getting more sunlight, which means that pockets of air are being warmed – those suddenly glorious spring days. But there are still also pockets of cold air. Cool air produces high-pressure areas, and warm air creates low-pressure areas. The warm air in a low-pressure area rises and, as it does so, the cooler air from a high-pressure area rushes in to replace it – creating wind. In effect, wind is just nature's attempt to even everything out and create an equilibrium.

Wind is pretty universally hated within the Romani community even now, particularly for its ability to overturn a wagon once it really gets strong. Even blustery gusts make wagon- and tent-living rather uncomfortable, as well as interfering with the functions of living out-of-doors. How do you cook outside when there is a gale blowing? How do you keep animals fed when hay gets blown away? So this is another month named after pesky weather, which is so immediate to those living close to nature. The Romani word *bavalesko* means 'of the wind' and *yakengeriengo* means 'of the clocks', so perhaps *bavalyakero* means something like 'wind time'.

Apart from when the gales are blowing, the countryside is a good place to be in March, after the chill of winter, with buds appearing on the hedgerows and spring flowers at their bases, and a handful of nutritious spring greens to pick alongside them: nettle tips, salad burnet and tansy. It would not have been unusual for Romani families to move on from the snowdrop woods to the daffodil fields where they could pick bunches, take them into town and sell them door to door.

# THE MOON

## Moon phases

3rd quarter – 6th March, 01.30

New moon – 13th March, 10.21

1st quarter – 21st March, 14.40

Full moon – 28th March, 19.48

## Gardening by the moon

**Full moon to 3rd quarter: 1st–6th and 28th–31st.** Harvest crops for immediate eating. Harvest fruit.

**3rd quarter to new moon: 6th–13th.** Prune. Harvest for storage. Fertilise and mulch the soil.

**New moon to 1st quarter: 13th–21st.** Sow crops that develop below ground. Dig the soil.

**1st quarter to full moon: 21st–28th.** Sow crops that develop above ground. Plant seedlings and young plants.

## Moon sign – Pisces

Astrologers believe that the new moon is a time to make plans and focus on your dreams and hopes for the period ahead, and that each new moon has a particular energy, depending on which zodiacal sign it is in. The new moon on the 13th will be in Pisces, which is said to be an intuitive sign, making this a good time to give space to your imagination and instincts, and to dream and heal.

### Navigating by the stars, sun and moon

### Make a star clock

Most of us have a good sense of roughly what time of day it is by the position of the sun, but with a bit of practice and a few calculations you can do the same with the night sky. Find the North Star, the Plough and the Plough's pointer stars Dubhe and Merak (see page 14), and then picture the North Star as the centre of a 24-hour, anticlockwise clock. The pointer line running between Dubhe and Merak will act as the hour hand.

This clock is set for 6th March: on this date, the line points straight up at midnight. Then add on 15 degrees anticlockwise for each hour. (Stretch out your arm, hold up your hand and spread your fingers. The space between your little finger and your forefinger will equal around 15 degrees in the sky.)

Beyond March you will need to do a simple calculation. Read the time, then take away two hours for every month you are past March. So if it's May and the clock reads 04.00, that would be 2 hours × 2 months, or midnight. You then need to add on one hour during British Summer Time, making it 01.00.

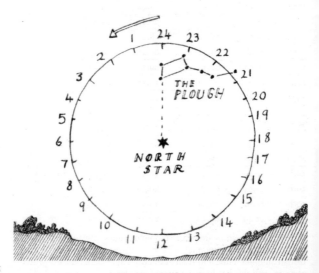

## Moon rise and set

| | St Michael's Mount | | Hopton-on-Sea | | |
|------|------|------|------|------|------|
| | Rise | Set | Rise | Set | |
| 1st | 20.57 | 08.25 | 20.28 | 07.56 | |
| 2nd | 22.21 | 08.44 | 21.54 | 08.13 | |
| 3rd | 23.44 | 09.05 | 23.21 | 08.31 | |
| 4th | — | 09.30 | — | 08.52 | |
| 5th | 01.08 | 09.59 | 00.47 | 09.19 | |
| 6th | 02.27 | 10.37 | 02.10 | 09.54 | 3rd quarter |
| 7th | 03.40 | 11.25 | 03.24 | 10.41 | |
| 8th | 04.40 | 12.25 | 04.25 | 11.40 | |
| 9th | 05.28 | 13.34 | 05.12 | 12.51 | |
| 10th | 06.04 | 14.47 | 05.46 | 14.06 | |
| 11th | 06.32 | 16.02 | 06.11 | 15.23 | |
| 12th | 06.54 | 17.15 | 06.31 | 16.39 | |
| 13th | 07.12 | 18.25 | 06.47 | 17.52 | new moon |
| 14th | 07.29 | 19.34 | 07.01 | 19.04 | |
| 15th | 07.44 | 20.42 | 07.14 | 20.14 | |
| 16th | 08.00 | 21.49 | 07.27 | 21.24 | |
| 17th | 08.17 | 22.57 | 07.42 | 22.34 | |
| 18th | 08.36 | — | 07.59 | 23.44 | |
| 19th | 09.00 | 00.04 | 08.20 | — | |
| 20th | 09.29 | 01.11 | 08.47 | 00.53 | |
| 21st | 10.07 | 02.14 | 09.23 | 01.58 | 1st quarter |
| 22nd | 10.55 | 03.12 | 10.10 | 02.57 | |
| 23rd | 11.54 | 04.03 | 11.10 | 03.47 | |
| 24th | 13.04 | 04.44 | 12.21 | 04.27 | |
| 25th | 14.21 | 05.17 | 13.41 | 04.58 | |
| 26th | 15.42 | 05.44 | 15.05 | 05.22 | |
| 27th | 17.05 | 06.07 | 16.31 | 05.42 | |
| 28th | 19.29 | 07.27 | 18.58 | 06.59 | full moon |
| 29th | 20.55 | 07.46 | 20.27 | 07.16 | |
| 30th | 22.22 | 08.07 | 21.57 | 07.34 | |
| 31st | 23.49 | 08.30 | 21.28 | 07.54 | |

Where moonset times are before moonrise times, this is the setting of the previous night's moon.
British Summer Time and Irish Standard Time begin on 28th March at 01.00, and this has been accounted for above.

# THE SKY

## At night

**19th:** Close approach of Mars and the moon, visible in the dusk from about 18.30 in the southwest, at an altitude of 52 degrees, until setting in the northwest at 00.30 on the 20th.

## By day

**20th:** The vernal equinox, or spring equinox, falls at 09.37. (The equinox is the moment when the sun is directly over the equator. The word comes from the Latin *aequi*, or 'equal', and *nox* or 'night'. Equinox occurs twice a year, in March and September.)

**21st:** At solar midday the sun reaches an altitude of 40 degrees at Lee-on-the-Solent in Hampshire and 32 degrees at Lairg in Scotland.

**31st:** Earliest sunrise, St Michael's Mount (07.00) and Hopton-on-Sea (06.29).

**31st:** Latest sunset, St Michael's Mount (19.52) and Hopton-on-Sea (19.26).

**1st–31st:** Daylight increases by 1h 53m at St Michael's Mount and by 1h 57m at Hopton-on-Sea.

## Sunrise and set

|       | St Michael's Mount | | Hopton-on-Sea | |
|-------|-------|-------|-------|-------|
|       | Rise  | Set   | Rise  | Set   |
| 1st   | 07.05 | 18.04 | 06.39 | 17.32 |
| 2nd   | 07.02 | 18.05 | 06.37 | 17.34 |
| 3rd   | 07.00 | 18.07 | 06.34 | 17.36 |
| 4th   | 06.58 | 18.09 | 06.32 | 17.37 |
| 5th   | 06.56 | 18.10 | 06.30 | 17.39 |
| 6th   | 06.54 | 18.12 | 06.28 | 17.41 |
| 7th   | 06.52 | 18.14 | 06.25 | 17.43 |
| 8th   | 06.50 | 18.15 | 06.23 | 17.45 |
| 9th   | 06.48 | 18.17 | 06.21 | 17.47 |
| 10th  | 06.46 | 18.18 | 06.18 | 17.48 |
| 11th  | 06.43 | 18.20 | 06.16 | 17.50 |
| 12th  | 06.41 | 18.22 | 06.14 | 17.52 |
| 13th  | 06.39 | 18.23 | 06.11 | 17.54 |
| 14th  | 06.37 | 18.25 | 06.09 | 17.56 |
| 15th  | 06.35 | 18.27 | 06.07 | 17.57 |
| 16th  | 06.33 | 18.28 | 06.04 | 17.59 |
| 17th  | 06.30 | 18.30 | 06.02 | 18.01 |
| 18th  | 06.28 | 18.31 | 06.00 | 18.13 |
| 19th  | 06.26 | 18.33 | 05.57 | 18.14 |
| 20th  | 06.24 | 18.35 | 05.55 | 18.16 |
| 21st  | 06.22 | 18.36 | 05.53 | 18.18 |
| 22nd  | 06.20 | 18.38 | 05.50 | 18.10 |
| 23rd  | 06.17 | 18.39 | 05.48 | 18.11 |
| 24th  | 06.15 | 18.41 | 05.46 | 18.13 |
| 25th  | 06.13 | 18.43 | 05.43 | 18.15 |
| 26th  | 06.11 | 18.44 | 05.41 | 18.17 |
| 27th  | 06.09 | 18.46 | 05.38 | 18.19 |
| 28th  | 07.06 | 19.47 | 06.36 | 19.20 |
| 29th  | 07.04 | 19.49 | 06.34 | 19.22 |
| 30th  | 07.02 | 19.50 | 06.31 | 19.24 |
| 31st  | 07.00 | 19.52 | 06.29 | 19.26 |

British Summer Time and Irish Standard Time begin on 28th March at 01.00, and this has been accounted for above.

# THE SEA

## Average sea temperature

| | |
|---|---:|
| Orkney: | 7.1°C |
| South Shields: | 6.8°C |
| Carrickfergus: | 8°C |
| Lowestoft: | 6.5°C |
| Aberystwyth: | 8.2°C |
| Bantry: | 10.1°C |
| Cowes: | 8.7°C |
| Penzance: | 9.4°C |

## Spring and neap tides

The spring tides are the most extreme tides of the month, with the highest rises and falls, and the neap tides are the least extreme, with the smallest. Exact timings vary around the coast, but expect them around the following dates:

**Spring tides:** 2nd–3rd, 15th–16th and 31st

**Neap tides:** 8th–9th and 23rd–24th

In the tide timetable opposite, spring tides are shown with an asterisk.

## March tide timetable for Dover

For guidance on how to convert this for your local area, see page 8.

| | High water | | Low water | |
| | Morning | Afternoon | Morning | Afternoon |
|---|---|---|---|---|
| 1st | 00.03 | 12.21 | 07.42 | 19.58 |
| 2nd | 00.43 | 13.00 | 08.22 | 20.34 * |
| 3rd | 01.23 | 13.41 | 08.59 | 21.10 * |
| 4th | 02.05 | 14.25 | 09.36 | 21.48 |
| 5th | 02.52 | 15.16 | 10.17 | 22.33 |
| 6th | 03.47 | 16.19 | 11.06 | 23.29 |
| 7th | 04.57 | 17.45 | — | 12.11 |
| 8th | 06.32 | 19.23 | 00.46 | 13.33 |
| 9th | 08.14 | 20.44 | 02.13 | 15.04 |
| 10th | 09.27 | 21.43 | 03.52 | 16.39 |
| 11th | 10.18 | 22.27 | 05.06 | 17.36 |
| 12th | 10.58 | 23.04 | 05.58 | 18.21 |
| 13th | 11.31 | 23.39 | 06.41 | 18.59 |
| 14th | — | 12.02 | 07.18 | 19.30 |
| 15th | 00.14 | 12.33 | 07.48 | 19.54 * |
| 16th | 00.47 | 13.02 | 08.11 | 20.13 * |
| 17th | 01.15 | 13.28 | 08.30 | 20.32 |
| 18th | 01.35 | 13.48 | 08.50 | 20.57 |
| 19th | 01.55 | 14.09 | 09.16 | 21.28 |
| 20th | 02.23 | 14.41 | 09.48 | 22.04 |
| 21st | 03.02 | 15.26 | 10.28 | 22.50 |
| 22nd | 03.58 | 17.32 | 11.24 | — |
| 23rd | 06.15 | 19.01 | 00.05 | 13.14 |
| 24th | 07.31 | 20.05 | 01.57 | 14.38 |
| 25th | 08.30 | 20.57 | 03.08 | 15.40 |
| 26th | 09.19 | 21.41 | 04.06 | 16.35 |
| 27th | 10.02 | 22.22 | 04.59 | 17.26 |
| 28th | 11.42 | - | 06.50 | 19.13 |
| 29th | 00.02 | 12.21 | 07.38 | 19.57 |
| 30th | 00.41 | 12.59 | 08.22 | 20.37 |
| 31st | 01.21 | 13.39 | 09.02 | 21.14 * |

British Summer Time and Irish Standard Time begin on 28th March at 01.00, and this has been accounted for above.

# A SEA SHANTY FOR MARCH

### The Gals o' Dublin Town

A shanty celebrating St Patrick's Day. Although shanties were also found further afield, the practice was strongly concentrated on the Atlantic merchant trading ships, with much cross-pollination of British, Irish and American songs, plus the songs of slaves and former slaves travelling from or working in the ports in the American South (of which more in October, page 210). New York and Dublin get a mention here, and British and Irish crews would have been quite used to sailing to New York – lucky them if they arrived on 17th March. It is another 'capstan' shanty (see page 42).

It was on a fa-mous Yan-kee ship to New York we were bound, and our
Cap-tain was an Ir-ish-man who came from Dub-lin Town, and
when he sees that bles-sed land, the town of high re-nown, it's
break a-way that green bur-gee and Harp with-out a Crown. Hurraw, hur-raw for the gals o' Dub-lin Town! Hur-
raw for the bon-nie green flag and the Harp with-out a Crown!

M

'Twas on the seventeenth of March we came to New York bay
And with the Irish union men we'd celebrate the day.
We'd fly aloft the Stars and Stripes a-flutterin' all around
But underneath his monkey-gaff, the Harp without the
    Crown.
*Hurraw, hurraw for the gals o' Dublin Town!*
*Hurraw for the bonnie green flag and the Harp without a*
    *Crown!*

Sometimes we are a happy lot, sometimes we'll sing a song,
Sometimes we wish we'd never been born, but don't complain
    for long,
And when the voyage is ended and we go back to shore
We'll say goodbye to the Yankee ship and go to sea no more.
*Hurraw...*

A MAP OF
TROYTOWN
LABYRINTH,
ST AGNES, THE ISLES OF SCILLY

# PILGRIMAGE OF THE MONTH

## St Agnes labyrinth

M

For this month, named by the Romanies for its gusty nature, the featured pilgrimage is a ritual journey to help sailors to tame storms before they leave shore. The Troy Town labyrinth on St Agnes, Isles of Scilly, is the only centuries-old stone labyrinth in the United Kingdom. Although it is rumoured to have been rebuilt by lighthouse keeper Amor Clarke in 1729, he may have done so on the site of a much older labyrinth, possibly a part of a larger Neolithic landscape. Clare Gogerty in her book *Beyond the Footpath* says that such labyrinths are frequently found on the shorelines of Sweden, Norway and Finland, often near ports, and that they were walked by fishermen before setting out to sea, to ensure a good catch and to ensnare unfavourable winds. The names of some of these labyrinths (Trojaborg, Troborg and Trojienborg) also allude to the defensive walls of Troy, which were built in a deliberately confusing and layered way.

Like the Scandinavian labyrinths, the one at Troy Town is a 'classical' labyrinth (one of the simplest and oldest kinds and the type associated with the myth of Theseus and the Minotaur). A classical labyrinth usually has seven circuits, as at Troy Town, but sometimes has eleven or fifteen. A labyrinth differs from a maze in that there is no possibility of getting lost – there is one route in and one route out. Therefore, the purpose is contemplative and ritualistic, like touching wood or crossing yourself at the thought of danger.

# THE GARDEN

### March garden meditation

Though the weather is still cold and the trees are still almost bare, there is so much happening in the garden that five minutes of reflection will reveal. Not least of these is the light – there is indeed a grand stretch in the evenings, and so dusk would be a good time to stand outside and feel the difference. Think about the equinox – the equality of night and day – and about the fact that the spot where you are standing on earth is gradually tilting back towards the sun. The birds feel it, too, and this month they start to warm up for the great crescendo of the dawn chorus in April and May. Early evening is a good time to hear blackbirds and robins testing their little lungs. As March is a breezy month, you may find yourself being buffeted by the wind. Don't resent it, it's only for five minutes – instead, close your eyes and feel how it swirls around you and plays with your hair.

Look to the delicate fuzz of green that is starting to appear on the trees, and think about the sap flowing up those gnarled and toughened trunks. It is waking them from their winter slumber, bringing the tips to green life so that they can unfold and tilt themselves towards the sun's ever-increasing energy.

**Jobs in the garden**

- Plant out an asparagus bed this month. Prepare and enrich the soil well before you do as you will be harvesting from it for many years to come.
- Feed your plants. Find a balanced organic fertiliser and water it around flowering plants in particular – roses, perennials and fruit bushes – to encourage greater flowering and fruiting this year.
- Spread compost or well-rotted manure over your beds, to hold in winter moisture and set the plants up for the growing season ahead.

**How much to sow**

It is tempting to sow whole packets of seeds and then be overwhelmed by seedlings or, later, great gluts of one type of vegetable. This guide will help you to sow roughly the amount you need for a family of four; adjust to suit your own circumstances and favourites. In every case, sow a small number more than suggested to allow for non-germination and seedling failure.

**Herbs:** Under glass or in a sheltered spot, fill a couple of seed trays with compost and sow a row each of herbs such as chives, coriander, dill, oregano and parsley, to prick out into individual pots in a month or so.

**Tomatoes:** Sow towards the end of the month, indoors in a heated propagator: ten plants of as many different varieties as you can manage.

**Winter squash:** This can be started in a heated propagator, too. Sow two plants each of two different varieties.

**Courgettes:** Start towards the end of the month, indoors, in the heated propagator if there is space: three plants of three varieties.

**Cucumber:** These should go into the heated propagator when there is room: three plants.

## THE KITCHEN

### Romani recipe for March – Gypsy spinach

Nettle tops are a free, nutritious green perfect at this time of year when still young and tender. Wear rubber gloves and gather just the tips. Heat removes the sting. Recipe based on the research of Romani and Traveller historian Robert Dawson.

Gather the tops of young nettles. Wash thoroughly. Cook with a little butter as one would spinach, until tender. Serve on bread fried in bacon fat.

### In season

### In the hedgerows, woods and fields
**Wild greens:** Alexanders, bistort, burdock, chickweed, comfrey leaves, dandelion, fat hen, Good-King-Henry, hawthorn tips, hop tips, nettle tips, orache, rampion, salad burnet, sea beet, sorrel, tansy, watercress, wild garlic, wintercress, wood sorrel
**Edible wild flowers:** Primulas, cowslips, violets
Birch sap
**Game:** Rabbit

### From the seashore and rivers
**Fish and shellfish:** Oysters, scallops, mussels, elvers, coley, dab, lemon sole, cod, haddock, whiting, pollock, salmon
**Seaweeds:** Laver, pepper dulse, carragheen, egg wrack, sea lettuce, sugar kelp, sea kale

### From the kitchen garden
**Vegetables:** Purple sprouting broccoli, Brussels sprouts, chicory, kale, onions, radishes, cabbages, cauliflowers, chard, endive, lettuce, spinach, turnips, forced rhubarb
**Herbs:** Sorrel, winter savory, parsley, chervil, coriander, rosemary, bay, sage

### From the farms
Fresh ewe's milk cheeses, Jersey Royal potatoes

## RECIPES

**Potato, sorrel and Cornish yarg pasty**

Although this is notionally included to celebrate St Piran's Day
on the 5th, it feels important to state that this is not a Cornish
pasty, before I bring down the wrath of Cornwall on my head.
It's just a pasty, containing some Cornish ingredients, that you
might eat around the 5th March if the urge took you. Good
packed for a day of bracing coastal walks, or tin mining.

| Makes 4 |
| --- |
| **Ingredients** |
| 1 large onion |
| 50g butter |
| 500g new potatoes, boiled and cut into cubes |
| 400g Cornish yarg cheese, cut into cubes |
| Handful of sorrel leaves, washed and chopped |
| 500g all butter shortcrust pastry block |
| 1 egg, beaten |
| Salt and pepper |

**Method**
Preheat the oven to 190°C/Gas Mark 5. Slice the onion
and cook in the butter until soft, translucent and slightly
caramelised. Tip into a bowl with the potatoes, cheese and
sorrel, season well with salt and pepper and mix thoroughly.
Divide the pastry into 4, form each into a ball and then roll out
each ball into a round on a floured surface. Divide the filling
between the 4 rounds, putting it on one half of the pastry
round. Paint the edges of the pastry with the beaten egg and
fold over and press to seal. Place them on a baking tray covered
in a sheet of baking parchment. Pierce the top of each pasty to
release steam as they cook, and then paint all with the beaten
egg. Bake for 35 minutes or until the pastry is crispy and
golden. Eat warm or leave to cool and pack for a picnic.

### Mothering Sunday wafers

The tradition of Mothering Sunday wafers harks back to the origins of the day, which, in fact, has nothing at all to do with mums. In the 16th century, Mid Lent Sunday became the time to travel home to visit your 'mother' church, the one where you were baptised. Pre-Reformation, offerings would be left on the altar, and among them were 'Mid Lent wafers'. A handy side effect of going to visit your mother church was a day off in your home village, where you could visit your actual mother, and so gradually the day took on its mum-celebrating meaning. The wafers moved out of church, too, and for a while were made and given as Mothering Sunday gifts, before the tradition faded away. Eat them as biscuits or with a creamy dessert (or tell your mum to).

| Makes 10–12 |
| --- |
| **Ingredients** |
| 2 tablespoons double cream |
| 2 tablespoons plain flour |
| 2 tablespoons caster sugar |
| 1 tablespoon orange flower water |

**Method**
Preheat the oven to 180°C/Gas Mark 4. Beat all of the ingredients together and pour into rounds on a parchment-lined baking tray. Bake for around 10 minutes, or until crisp.

# MIGRATION OF THE MONTH

M

### Bewick's swan migration

While we mostly see returnees at this time of year – creatures that have spent winter somewhere warmer – the hardy and elegant Bewick's swans are about to leave us. These are the smallest swans that visit our islands, the adults pure white with a yellow and black bill and the juveniles grey with a soft pink bill. Their call is gentle and musical, markedly different from the comedy honk of whooper swans. Bewick's swans use their voices often, making a range of different noises for different purposes: pre-flight, while flying, to locate each other, to threaten, to mark out territory and undoubtedly much more.

There are three distinct groups of Bewick's swans, and those that overwinter in the United Kingdom and Ireland are the northwest European population, which in summer breed on moss-lichen tundra near shallow pools and lakes to the west of the Ural Mountains in the Russian Arctic. Cold, yes, but relatively predator-free and with almost constant daylight for foraging. But winter is a different matter. In comparison with the Arctic, our winter weather is a luxury. They overwinter on our freshwater wetlands – reedbeds, wet grasslands, fens and bogs – and frequent farmland by day to pick over the leavings of last year's crops, feasting on sugar beet, potatoes and wheat stubble before returning to the water to roost at night.

Bewick's swans mate for life – one pair has returned to Slimbridge Wetland Centre in Gloucestershire every year for 19 years, bringing 29 cygnets. They travel in family groups, teaching the cygnets the route, and if separated will seek each other out and perform a joyful dance on reuniting. Extended family groups of parents, siblings and even grandchildren will honk joyfully when they find themselves together. Now that winter is over, it is time for them to group together and head off to their breeding grounds. It is a long and treacherous journey of up to 5,600km, with hunters, power lines and predators to avoid. Hopefully it will be a successful one this year, and the Bewick's families will be reunited again next winter.

# April

 April Fools' Day

Good Friday (Christian) – bank holiday, England, Wales, Scotland, Northern Ireland

 Easter Sunday (Christian)

Easter Monday – bank holiday, England, Wales, Northern Ireland and Republic of Ireland

 Yom Hashoah – Holocaust Remembrance Day (Jewish) – begins at sunset the previous night

Grand National

 First day of Ramadan (Muslim) – begins at the sighting of the new moon the evening before

 Earth Day

St George's Day – patron saint of England

Start of British asparagus season

Shakespeare Day – William Shakespeare's birthday

 Orthodox Good Friday (Orthodox)

# ROMANI NAME FOR THE MONTH

## Brishindeskero – month of the rains

April is a month of sunshine and showers: clear blue, perfect skies which then fill with big, fat cumulonimbus clouds; bright, lemony sunshine and hefty cloudbursts. It is no wonder then that the Romani name for April means 'month of the rains'. These sudden soakings would have been tricky to manage for people essentially living, cooking and working out-of-doors. If the women and children were out collecting bunches of spring flowers from along the hedgerow bottoms, and then bundling them up and taking them into towns to sell them door to door, they would have been in for a thorough soaking, and that would make the rest of the day hard to bear.

The reason for all these showers is a similar atmospheric discrepancy to that which caused all of those windy gusts in March. The sun is hitting the ground at an ever-steeper angle and so the land has started to warm up all around us, but the great thermal mass of the sea lags behind, clinging on to the chill of January and February. Warm air can hold more water vapour than cold air, and where warm air and cold air collide (creating a 'front'), the warm air rises over the cold air, which causes the warm air to cool and the moisture to condense, forming great rain-filled clouds.

Despite this, taken as a whole April is actually one of our drier months, but there is no contradiction in the fact that we all think of it as rainy. April clouds typically move fast, blown along by spring breezes, often through otherwise blue skies. They drop their load dramatically, in a quick, drenching shower that gives little time to run to shelter, and then are whisked away. Although this may have made it a slightly trying time to be living out-of-doors, April has plenty in its favour. The landscape is warming and coming to life, the first butterflies flitting, the birds singing and the flowers starting to bloom. Moving at horse's pace through flower-sprinkled country lanes coming to life before your eyes might have been worth the odd soaking.

# THE MOON

## Moon phases

3rd quarter – 4th April, 11.02

New moon – 12th April, 03.31

1st quarter – 20th April, 07.59

Full moon – 27th April, 04.32*

## Gardening by the moon

**Full moon to 3rd quarter: 1st–4th and 27th–30th.** Harvest crops for immediate eating. Harvest fruit.

**3rd quarter to new moon: 4th–12th.** Prune. Harvest for storage. Fertilise and mulch the soil.

**New moon to 1st quarter: 12th–20th.** Sow crops that develop below ground. Dig the soil.

**1st quarter to full moon: 20th–27th.** Sow crops that develop above ground. Plant seedlings and young plants.

## Moon sign – Aries

Astrologers believe that the new moon is a time to make plans and focus on your dreams and hopes for the period ahead, and that each new moon has a particular energy, depending on which zodiacal sign it is in. The new moon on the 12th will be in Aries, which is said to be an active and courageous sign, making this a good time for creativity and fun.

*This month the full moon falls in the early hours of the morning. To see the moon at its fullest within normal waking hours, view it the evening before the date given above.

### Navigating by the stars, sun and moon

#### Use the crescent moon

There are a few ways of using the moon to tell direction, and this is the simplest. It's not particularly accurate but will give you a rough reading. The crescent moon can be used to point to south when viewed in the northern hemisphere (and north when viewed from the southern). Draw an imaginary line between the two points of the crescent, and extend it down to the ground. Where it meets the ground will be south, or thereabouts, and will be more accurate when the moon is not too close to the horizon. This works because the sun and moon follow the same path east to west across the sky, so the sun is always east or west of the moon (except at new moon when they are in step). As the moon is just the reflected light of the sun, the crescent moon will always be pointing towards the east or west, and the imaginary line is perpendicular to this and so points to south.

SOUTH

## Moon rise and set

| | St Michael's Mount | | Hopton-on-Sea | | |
|------|------|------|------|------|------|
| | Rise | Set | Rise | Set | |
| 1st | — | 08.58 | — | 08.19 | |
| 2nd | 01.14 | 09.34 | 00.56 | 08.51 | |
| 3rd | 02.32 | 10.19 | 02.16 | 09.35 | |
| 4th | 03.38 | 11.17 | 03.23 | 10.32 | 3rd quarter |
| 5th | 04.30 | 12.24 | 04.14 | 11.40 | |
| 6th | 05.09 | 13.37 | 04.51 | 12.55 | |
| 7th | 05.38 | 14.51 | 05.18 | 14.11 | |
| 8th | 06.01 | 16.03 | 05.39 | 15.27 | |
| 9th | 06.20 | 17.14 | 05.55 | 16.40 | |
| 10th | 06.36 | 18.23 | 06.09 | 17.52 | |
| 11th | 06.51 | 19.31 | 06.22 | 19.02 | |
| 12th | 07.06 | 20.38 | 06.35 | 20.12 | new moon |
| 13th | 07.22 | 21.46 | 06.48 | 21.22 | |
| 14th | 07.40 | 22.53 | 07.04 | 22.32 | |
| 15th | 08.02 | — | 07.23 | 23.42 | |
| 16th | 08.29 | 00.00 | 07.47 | — | |
| 17th | 09.03 | 01.05 | 08.19 | 00.49 | |
| 18th | 09.46 | 02.06 | 09.01 | 01.50 | |
| 19th | 10.40 | 02.58 | 09.55 | 02.43 | |
| 20th | 11.44 | 03.42 | 11.01 | 03.26 | 1st quarter |
| 21st | 12.56 | 04.17 | 12.15 | 03.59 | |
| 22nd | 14.14 | 04.45 | 13.35 | 04.25 | |
| 23rd | 15.34 | 05.09 | 14.58 | 04.45 | |
| 24th | 16.56 | 05.29 | 16.24 | 05.03 | |
| 25th | 18.21 | 05.48 | 17.52 | 05.20 | |
| 26th | 19.48 | 06.08 | 19.22 | 05.36 | |
| 27th | 21.18 | 06.29 | 20.54 | 05.55 | full moon |
| 28th | 22.47 | 06.55 | 22.28 | 06.17 | |
| 29th | — | 07.27 | 23.56 | 06.46 | |
| 30th | 00.12 | 08.09 | — | 07.25 | |

Where moonset times are before moonrise times, this is the setting of the previous night's moon.

# THE SKY

## At night

**17th:** Close approach of a dim Mars and the moon, visible in the dusk from about 20.00 in the southwest at an altitude of 43 degrees, until setting at 01.00 on the 18th in the northwest.

## By day

**21st:** At solar midday (approximately 13.00 BST/IST) the sun reaches an altitude of 51 degrees at Lee-on-the-Solent in Hampshire and 44 degrees at Lairg in Scotland.

**30th:** Earliest sunrise, St Michael's Mount (05.59) and Hopton-on-Sea (05.23).

**30th:** Latest sunset, St Michael's Mount (20.39) and Hopton-on-Sea (20.18).

**1st–30th:** Daylight increases by 1h 45m at St Michael's Mount and by 1h 54m at Hopton-on-Sea.

**Sunrise and set**

|  | St Michael's Mount | | Hopton-on-Sea | |
|---|---|---|---|---|
|  | Rise | Set | Rise | Set |
| 1st | 06.58 | 19.54 | 06.27 | 19.27 |
| 2nd | 06.56 | 19.55 | 06.24 | 19.29 |
| 3rd | 06.53 | 19.57 | 06.22 | 19.31 |
| 4th | 06.51 | 19.58 | 06.20 | 19.33 |
| 5th | 06.49 | 20.00 | 06.17 | 19.34 |
| 6th | 06.47 | 20.02 | 06.15 | 19.36 |
| 7th | 06.45 | 20.03 | 06.13 | 19.38 |
| 8th | 06.43 | 20.05 | 06.11 | 19.40 |
| 9th | 06.41 | 20.06 | 06.08 | 19.41 |
| 10th | 06.38 | 20.08 | 06.06 | 19.43 |
| 11th | 06.36 | 20.09 | 06.04 | 19.45 |
| 12th | 06.34 | 20.11 | 06.01 | 19.47 |
| 13th | 06.32 | 20.13 | 05.59 | 19.48 |
| 14th | 06.30 | 20.14 | 05.57 | 19.50 |
| 15th | 06.28 | 20.16 | 05.55 | 19.52 |
| 16th | 06.26 | 20.17 | 05.52 | 19.54 |
| 17th | 06.24 | 20.19 | 05.50 | 19.55 |
| 18th | 06.22 | 20.20 | 05.48 | 19.57 |
| 19th | 06.20 | 20.22 | 05.46 | 19.59 |
| 20th | 06.18 | 20.24 | 05.44 | 20.01 |
| 21st | 06.16 | 20.25 | 05.42 | 20.02 |
| 22nd | 06.14 | 20.27 | 05.39 | 20.04 |
| 23rd | 06.12 | 20.28 | 05.37 | 20.06 |
| 24th | 06.10 | 20.30 | 05.35 | 20.07 |
| 25th | 06.08 | 20.31 | 05.33 | 20.09 |
| 26th | 06.06 | 20.33 | 05.31 | 20.11 |
| 27th | 06.05 | 20.35 | 05.29 | 20.13 |
| 28th | 06.03 | 20.36 | 05.27 | 20.14 |
| 29th | 06.01 | 20.38 | 05.25 | 20.16 |
| 30th | 05.59 | 20.39 | 05.23 | 20.18 |

A

# THE SEA

## Average sea temperature

| | |
|---|---:|
| Orkney: | 7.8°c |
| South Shields: | 8.2°c |
| Carrickfergus: | 8.8°c |
| Lowestoft: | 8.3°c |
| Aberystwyth: | 9.2°c |
| Bantry: | 10.7°c |
| Cowes: | 9.8°c |
| Penzance: | 10.4°c |

## Spring and neap tides

The spring tides are the most extreme tides of the month, with the highest rises and falls, and the neap tides are the least extreme, with the smallest. Exact timings vary around the coast, but expect them around the following dates:

**Spring tides:** 1st, 14th–15th and 28th–30th

**Neap tides:** 6th–7th and 21st–22nd

In the tide timetable opposite, spring tides are shown with an asterisk.

**April tide timetable for Dover**

For guidance on how to convert this for your local area, see page 8.

| | High water | | Low water | |
| | Morning | Afternoon | Morning | Afternoon |
| --- | --- | --- | --- | --- |
| 1st | 02.02 | 14.21 | 09.39 | 21.51 * |
| 2nd | 02.45 | 15.07 | 10.17 | 22.31 |
| 3rd | 03.34 | 16.00 | 10.58 | 23.16 |
| 4th | 04.31 | 17.04 | 11.47 | — |
| 5th | 05.42 | 18.24 | 00.15 | 12.56 |
| 6th | 07.19 | 20.02 | 01.34 | 14.22 |
| 7th | 09.10 | 21.27 | 03.07 | 15.58 |
| 8th | 10.15 | 22.22 | 04.44 | 17.18 |
| 9th | 11.00 | 23.04 | 05.47 | 18.11 |
| 10th | 11.36 | 23.41 | 06.35 | 18.53 |
| 11th | — | 12.07 | 07.16 | 19.28 |
| 12th | 00.15 | 12.36 | 07.49 | 19.57 |
| 13th | 00.49 | 13.06 | 08.15 | 20.20 |
| 14th | 01.19 | 13.34 | 08.35 | 20.39 * |
| 15th | 01.45 | 13.57 | 08.55 | 21.02 * |
| 16th | 02.01 | 14.14 | 09.19 | 21.30 |
| 17th | 02.21 | 14.37 | 09.47 | 22.02 |
| 18th | 02.51 | 15.12 | 10.19 | 22.38 |
| 19th | 03.31 | 15.58 | 10.59 | 23.23 |
| 20th | 04.26 | 17.18 | 11.50 | — |
| 21st | 06.42 | 19.22 | 00.29 | 13.19 |
| 22nd | 07.59 | 20.29 | 02.17 | 15.02 |
| 23rd | 09.00 | 21.23 | 03.32 | 16.06 |
| 24th | 09.50 | 22.10 | 04.32 | 17.01 |
| 25th | 10.34 | 22.53 | 05.27 | 17.54 |
| 26th | 11.16 | 23.35 | 06.21 | 18.44 |
| 27th | 11.57 | — | 07.12 | 19.31 |
| 28th | 00.17 | 12.38 | 07.59 | 20.14 * |
| 29th | 00.59 | 13.20 | 08.42 | 20.56 * |
| 30th | 01.43 | 14.05 | 09.22 | 21.36 * |

# A SEA SHANTY FOR APRIL

## A Wife in Every Port

A song for the month of the rains. While wind and gales are frequently mentioned in sea shanties, rain is not, presumably because a bit of rain is nothing when you have massive waves crashing over the deck and soaking you through. But here rain gets a mention, perhaps just to underline how very hard our sailor has worked to get back to his lassie. Despite these heroics and as the title suggests, no one comes out of this tale looking good, though likewise the outcome might well suit all quite nicely.

This appears to be a shanty for heaving jobs, possibly used for capstan and pump (see page 42). As it is a 'homeward bounder' (a song that mentions home) it might have been an 'anchor song', for keeping time when raising or lowering the anchor.

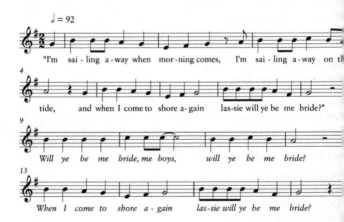

♩ = 92

"I'm sai-ling a-way when mor-ning comes, I'm sai-ling a-way on the tide, and when I come to shore a-gain las-sie will ye be me bride?"

Will ye be me bride, me boys, will ye be me bride?

When I come to shore a-gain las-sie will ye be me bride?

'Laddie, I will wait for you
As long as all me life.
Laddie, I will wait for you
I'll be a sailor's wife.'
*I'll be a sailor's wife, me boys,*
*I'll be a sailor's wife*
*Laddie, I will wait for you*
*I'll be a sailor's wife.*

The sun it shone and wind it blew
And the ship sailed out to sea,
When she caught the eye of a soldier lad
Standing on the quay.
*Standing on the quay, me boys,*
*Standing on the quay*
*She caught the eye of a soldier lad*
*Standing on the quay.*

The wind it blew and the cannons roared
and driving was the rain,
After twelve long months at sea
He was homeward bound again.
*Homeward bound again, me boys,*
*Homeward bound again*
*After twelve long months at sea*
*He was homeward bound again.*

And there he met her at the docks
With a baby in her arms
Saying, 'I am sorry, sailor lad,
But I fell for a soldier's charms.'
*Fell for a soldier's charms, me boys,*
*Fell for a soldier's charms*
*I am sorry, sailor lad,*
*But I fell for a soldier's charms.*

'Don't you fret me bonnie lass'
Was the sailor's bold retort,
'Don't you fret me bonnie lass,
I've a wife in every port!'
*Wife in every port, me boys,*
*Wife in every port*
*Don't you fret me bonnie lass,*
*I've a wife in every port!*

RUSSIA

BRITAIN

NOVEMBER

BELGIUM

UKRAINE

APRIL

AUSTRIA

A MAP OF
. WOODCOCK .
MIGRATION

# MIGRATION OF THE MONTH

## Woodcock

On the cusp of March and April, the woodcocks set off under the silvery light of the moon, answering the call to return to their breeding grounds. These elusive birds, with their rounded brown bodies, thin bills and long waders' legs, are crepuscular. That is, they are out and about hunting for food at dawn and dusk, and then they roost in woodland trees during the day. Woodcocks have spent the winter here in boggy areas, in woodland or on river plains, their beautiful brown speckled plumage camouflaging them against the undergrowth, while feasting themselves on the small invertebrates they pull from soft ground and mud with their slender beaks. This good living has allowed them to put on the fat reserves that will see them through their long flight east. Now it is time for them to lift into the moonlit air with the erratic flight path that makes them such a challenge for hunters, who will have routinely missed them all through the winter hunting season, but considered them quite the prize when they occasionally lucked out and hit their target.

While around 55,000 woodcocks are resident in Britain and Ireland all year round, their population is boosted by around 1.5 million over winter by migrants from Scandinavia, Finland, the Baltic states, western Russia and Siberia. But they have seen out the frozen months now, and it is time for them all to leave Britain, heading back to their summer breeding grounds. There they will carry out a courtship display called 'roding', the females encouraging their suitors by flying over them and flashing their white tail feathers at them. But for now, the long journey is the thing. (One particular woodcock, satellite-tagged in Cornwall by the Game & Wildlife Conservation Trust, made its spring migration via Austria to Russia, where it bred, and then returned in the autumn via Ukraine and Belgium.) The woodcocks will return in November, and November's full moon is known as the 'Woodcock Moon' because they so often coincide with it.

# THE GARDEN

## April garden meditation

Plenty of showers but also lots of sunshine is associated with April, and with a bit of luck you will experience one or the other if you step outside and turn your face to the sky for five minutes. Take your shoes and socks off if you dare and think about the earth warming beneath your toes. Imagine how the seas all around us are still cold, clinging on to that winter chill. Look closely at the rain and the raindrops. In some places they will have turned whole leaves slick and shining; in others they'll have formed pearls that wobble and then roll off at the slightest touch. Look for your best rain plant. Observe all the shades of green you can see and try to name them: lime? emerald? moss? Notice the bees and insects visiting the blossom and the spring flowers. See them through the insects' eyes as they are lured in by their beauty and scent and the nectar they hold. And then think about the switch that those insects trip, which sets into motion a whole summer's worth of forming, swelling and ripening. That process is now beginning all around you.

## Jobs in the garden

- Mow your lawn and trim around the edges to tidy it up. If your edges have got very messy you can sharpen them up with a half-moon lawn edger, cutting along a string line.
- Plant out sweet pea seedlings at the base of a wigwam of poles tied together at the top with string, and with twine spiralled around and tied to the canes at 1-m intervals.
- Plant your potatoes into the bottom of a trench, then mound soil over them. You will need to be ready to mound them up further as growth appears, in order to encourage the most potatoes to form.

A

## How much to sow

It is tempting to sow whole packets of seeds and then be overwhelmed by seedlings or, later, great gluts of one type of vegetable. This guide will help you to sow roughly the amount you need for a family of four; adjust to suit your own circumstances and favourites. In every case, sow a small number more than suggested to allow for non-germination and seedling failure.

**Beetroot and carrot:** Sow a 3-m row of each direct into the ground, covering the carrots with fleece.

**Mixed salad leaves:** Broadcast sow a wide seed drill about 1m long for a cut-and-come-again crop.

**Radishes and spring onions:** Direct sow a 1-m row of each.

**Spinach and Swiss chard:** Direct sow a 3-m row of each.

**Runner beans and French beans:** Erect cane supports and direct sow a 3-m row of runner beans and a 3-m row of French beans (or dwarf French beans without supports).

**Leeks:** Sow two 4-m rows of two different varieties.

**Sweetcorn and Florence fennel:** Sow 20 plants of sweetcorn and 10 plants of Florence fennel, under cover, to plant out next month.

**Parsnip:** Direct sow a 3-m row.

# THE KITCHEN

### Romani recipe for April – Egg balls

Hens start laying abundantly around now and this is a good use for any excess eggs – a sort of boiled egg and onion croquette. Recipe based on the research of Romani and Traveller historian Robert Dawson.

Hard-boil 4 eggs, then peel and chop them finely. In a frying pan melt 60g butter and stir in 60g plain flour, cooking slowly until it takes on a sandy look. Slowly add 400ml full fat milk, stirring all the time until it thickens enough to come away from the edges of the pot. Add the chopped eggs, a handful of chopped parsley and a quarter of an onion, finely chopped. Season and leave to cool. Mould into balls, dip into a batter of flour and water, and deep-fry.

### In season

### In the hedgerows, woods and fields
**Wild greens:** Alexanders, beech leaves, bistort, burdock, chickweed, comfrey leaves, dandelion, fat hen, Good-King-Henry, hawthorn tips, hop tips, nettle tips, orache, rampion, salad burnet, sea beet, sorrel, tansy, watercress, wintercress, wood sorrel
**Edible wild flowers:** Cowslips, violets, broom
**Roots:** Wild garlic

### From the seashore and rivers
**Fish and shellfish:** Brown crab, sea trout, turbot, elvers, lobster, halibut, salmon, shrimp, whitebait
**Seaweeds:** Laver, pepper dulse, carragheen, egg wrack, sea lettuce, sugar kelp, sea kale

### From the kitchen garden
**Vegetables:** Asparagus, purple sprouting broccoli, cauliflower, chard, endive, lettuce, spring onions, radishes, spinach, turnips, cabbages, spring greens, rhubarb
**Herbs:** Sorrel, parsley, chervil, coriander

### From the farms
Fresh ewe's milk cheeses, Jersey Royal potatoes, asparagus

# RECIPES

### Ribboned asparagus, carrot and radish salad with chopped egg tartare sauce

British asparagus season arrives this month, starting on 23rd April and running for eight short weeks, at which point the growers stop cutting and allow the spears to grow out into all their ferny beauty. It will all be over by the summer solstice, so make the most of it while you can.

When asparagus is young and squeaky, this is a lovely way to eat it. Mandolined, it becomes a piece of art, the tips like the roof of a canalside house in Amsterdam. The sauce goes very nicely with steamed asparagus, too.

| Serves 4 |
| --- |
| **Ingredients** |
| 4 small carrots, cleaned, topped and tailed |
| 6 spears of asparagus, ends snapped off |
| 8 radishes, cleaned, topped and tailed |
| 4 tablespoons extra virgin olive oil |
| Juice of half a lemon |
| |
| *For the sauce* |
| 2 eggs |
| 200g mayonnaise |
| 3 tablespoons capers, chopped |
| 3 tablespoons gherkins |
| 1 shallot, finely diced |
| 1 tablespoon finely chopped dill |
| 1 tablespoon finely chopped parsley |
| Juice of half a lemon |
| Salt and pepper |

### Method

Use a mandolin to very carefully make lengthwise slivers of all of the vegetables. Take your time and don't rush, as it is so easy to hurt yourself. Put them all into a bowl with the oil, lemon juice and salt and pepper. Toss them together, then set them aside to marinate and soften while you make the sauce.

Boil the eggs for 8 minutes and leave to cool. Chop them roughly and mix with the remaining sauce ingredients.

Divide the vegetables between plates and add a dollop of sauce to each. This is good with a hunk of soft bread.

A

### Saffron, cardamom, chocolate and apricot sticky buns

Saffron has long been associated with Easter baking and these sticky buns – rich in Lent-antagonistic butter, eggs, sugar and chocolate – make a beautiful and indulgent Easter Sunday breakfast.

Start them the day before as they need a slow rise, and bake them in the morning to enjoy them hot from the oven in a shaft of sunlight alongside your Easter eggs, pots of steaming coffee and vases full of daffodils.

### Makes 8

### Ingredients

A good pinch of saffron strands

175ml full fat milk

1 ½ teaspoons quick yeast

75g caster sugar

4 cardamom pods

500g strong white flour

2 eggs, beaten

75g butter, softened

Pinch of salt

200g 70%-cocoa plain dark chocolate

200g dried apricots

1 tablespoon golden syrup

### Method

Put the saffron strands in a few teaspoons of warm water and leave to soak for at least half an hour. Warm the milk, scoop out a cupful and add the yeast and a spoonful of the sugar. Mix and leave to activate, until you see bubbles forming on the top. Bash the cardamom pods in a pestle and mortar, then remove the papery husks and grind the seeds until fine.

Put the flour and remaining sugar into a mixing bowl, and tip in the warm milk, yeast mixture, saffron mixture, beaten eggs, softened butter and salt. Mix until all comes together into a dough, then tip out onto a floured surface and knead for 10 minutes. Place in a clean bowl, cover with a tea towel, and leave to rise in a warm place for 1–2 hours or until doubled in size.

Grease a baking tray with butter and put it aside. Roughly chop the chocolate and the apricots. Tip the dough onto a floured surface and stretch it out, then sprinkle the chocolate and apricots over it. Fold, knead and stretch the dough until the chocolate and apricots are well mixed in. Split the dough into 8 pieces and roll each into a ball. Place them on the buttered tray with a little space between them (though it won't matter if they meet and join up mid-bake). Cover with a tea towel, then leave to rise in a warm place for an hour, or cover with clingfilm and leave overnight in the fridge if you want to bake them in the morning.

If you have refrigerated the buns overnight, remove from the fridge at least an hour before you want to bake them so that they can come back to room temperature.

Preheat the oven to 180°C/Gas Mark 4 and bake for 35 minutes, or until golden all over. Remove from the oven and leave to cool on the tray for about 5 minutes. Warm the golden syrup and paint the buns all over. Eat immediately while still warm, or toast later.

# PILGRIMAGE OF THE MONTH

## Kumbh mela

Once, long ago, the gods and demons of Hindu legend fought a great battle, the Samudra Manthan, over a pot of Amrita, the nectar of immortality. In this fight four drops were spilt, one each on the cities of Allahabad (where the rivers Ganges and Yamuna converge), Haridwar (on the Ganges river), Nashik (on the Godavari river) and Ujjain (on the Kshipra river). Every 12 years, each of these cities plays host to the Kumbh Mela – the timings are determined by the relative positions of Jupiter, the sun and the moon, but it takes place on 4 occasions during the 12-year period. Millions of Hindu devotees, including a great number from Britain and Ireland, gather together to bathe in the river waters, as doing so on these auspicious days grants freedom from the cycle of life and rebirth, and allows the attainment of Prayascitta, atonement for past sins. It is the world's largest pilgrimage and greatest gathering of people, with up to 120 million pilgrims visiting the largest Kumbhs at Allahabad.

This year it is the turn of Haridwar, on the Ganges, the dates determined by Jupiter moving into Aquarius and the sun into Aries. The Haridwar Kumbh began in January and lasts 51 days, but the most auspicious day for bathing, the Amavasya, falls on 12th April, coinciding with the new moon. This day draws the greatest number of bathers.

Hinduism has a long history in Britain, the first wave of Hindus arriving from India following British India's independence and partition in 1947. All rivers are considered sacred by Hindus, and in the UK the Thames has become a kind of substitute river for offerings by members of the Anglo–Hindu community who cannot reach the Ganges. Sacred objects are released into its flowing waters to energise them and release their powers, and many statues of gods are deposited in the Thames throughout the year, in particular statues of Ganesh, elephant god and remover of obstacles.

MAY

MONTH OF THE HAWTHORN

PARNE-KARESKERO

V

# May

**1** May Day (traditional)

**1** Beltane (Gaelic/pagan/neopagan)

**1** International Workers' Day

**2** Orthodox Easter Sunday (Orthodox)

**3** Early May bank holiday, England, Wales, Scotland and Northern Ireland

**3** May Day bank holiday, Republic of Ireland

**8** Laylat al Qadr – the Night of Power (Muslim)

**9** Rogation Sunday, beating the bounds (Christian/traditional)

**13** Ascension Day, Holy Thursday (Christian)

**13** Eid al-Fitr – celebration of the end of Ramadan (Muslim) – celebrations begin at sundown the evening before

**14** Stow Horse Fair – spring Gypsy, Romani and Traveller gathering

**17** Feast of Weeks, Shavuot (Jewish) – celebrations begin at sundown the evening before

**23** Whit Sunday/Whitsun/Pentecost (Christian)

**30** Trinity Sunday (Christian)

**31** Spring/Late May bank holiday, England, Wales, Scotland and Northern Ireland

# ROMANI NAME FOR THE MONTH

### Parne-kareskero – month of the hawthorn

The great froth of hawthorn blossom that lines almost every field this month would be enough to warrant naming the month after it. It is one of the natural wonders of the year, and the moment the May flowers burst open, summer feels very surely on its way. But hawthorn also had several important functions for the Romani at the time these names were widely used. May flower buds were traditionally eaten and it was said that they prevented illness for the rest of the year; perhaps they provided some boost of vitamins that had been lacking in the diet over the winter. A hawthorn was customarily planted on the top of a roadside burial, and the tree's thorns were used to make tent pins during the days before 'wagon time', when the Romanies started living in wagons, though the stronger, sharper thorns of blackthorn were preferred.

In addition to Parne-kareskero, or 'month of the hawthorn', a second Romani language name for the month is Bakichengero, which means 'month of the lambs'. Though the Romani have followed the need for agricultural labour, there is no great tradition of joining in with lambing, though it is possible that those with links to particular farmers might have been involved. The name is more likely to be an observation of what can be seen this month as you travel through the countryside, and an acknowledgement of the cycle of life starting up again. So, in a month when the hedgerows are full of hawthorn flower and the fields full of lambs, with gentle weather, increasing sunshine and ever-improving prospects for agricultural work and money, it's hardly surprising that this is the first month of the year that's not named after fearsome weather. May is for the living.

# THE MOON

## Moon phases

3rd quarter – 3rd May, 20.50

New moon – 11th May, 20.00

1st quarter – 19th May, 20.13

Full moon – 26th May, 12.14

## Gardening by the moon

**Full moon to 3rd quarter: 1st–3rd and 26th–31st.** Harvest crops for immediate eating. Harvest fruit.

**3rd quarter to new moon: 3rd–11th.** Prune. Harvest for storage. Fertilise and mulch the soil.

**New moon to 1st quarter: 11th–19th.** Sow crops that develop below ground. Dig the soil.

**1st quarter to full moon: 19th–26th.** Sow crops that develop above ground. Plant seedlings and young plants.

## Moon sign – Taurus

Astrologers believe that the new moon is a time to make plans and focus on your dreams and hopes for the period ahead, and that each new moon has a particular energy, depending on which zodiacal sign it is in. The new moon on the 11th will be in Taurus, which is said to be an earthy and steady sign, making this a good time for planning projects of a practical nature.

### Navigating by the stars, sun and moon

**Find east and west using the moon**

The moon can give you navigational clues if you know
whether it is waxing or waning. When it is waxing – that is,
from new moon, through first quarter, to full – the lit side
will be facing towards the west, as at that point in its cycle it
is following the sun across the sky towards sunset in the west.
When it is waning – from full moon, through third quarter, to
new moon – the lit side faces east, as at that point in the cycle
it is being chased across the sky ahead of the rising sun. 'West'
is when the right side is more lit up, and when more shadow is
on the left side than the right side; 'east' is when the left side
is more lit up.

WAXING MOON

WANING MOON

## Moon rise and set

| | St Michael's Mount | | Hopton-on-Sea | | |
|---|---|---|---|---|---|
| | Rise | Set | Rise | Set | |
| 1st | 01.27 | 09.04 | 01.12 | 08.19 | |
| 2nd | 02.26 | 10.11 | 02.12 | 09.25 | |
| 3rd | 03.11 | 11.24 | 02.54 | 10.41 | 3rd quarter |
| 4th | 03.43 | 12.39 | 03.25 | 11.59 | |
| 5th | 04.08 | 13.53 | 03.47 | 13.16 | |
| 6th | 04.28 | 15.05 | 04.04 | 14.30 | |
| 7th | 04.44 | 16.14 | 04.18 | 15.42 | |
| 8th | 05.00 | 17.21 | 04.31 | 16.52 | |
| 9th | 05.14 | 18.29 | 04.43 | 18.01 | |
| 10th | 05.30 | 19.36 | 04.56 | 19.11 | |
| 11th | 05.47 | 20.44 | 05.11 | 20.22 | new moon |
| 12th | 06.07 | 21.51 | 05.28 | 21.32 | |
| 13th | 06.31 | 22.58 | 05.51 | 22.41 | |
| 14th | 07.02 | — | 06.19 | 23.44 | |
| 15th | 07.42 | 00.00 | 06.58 | — | |
| 16th | 08.33 | 00.55 | 07.47 | 00.40 | |
| 17th | 09.33 | 01.41 | 08.49 | 01.26 | |
| 18th | 10.41 | 02.19 | 09.59 | 02.02 | |
| 19th | 11.55 | 02.48 | 11.15 | 02.29 | 1st quarter |
| 20th | 13.12 | 03.12 | 12.35 | 02.50 | |
| 21st | 14.30 | 03.33 | 13.56 | 03.08 | |
| 22nd | 15.51 | 03.52 | 15.20 | 03.24 | |
| 23rd | 17.15 | 04.10 | 16.47 | 03.40 | |
| 24th | 18.42 | 04.30 | 18.17 | 03.57 | |
| 25th | 20.11 | 04.52 | 19.50 | 04.16 | |
| 26th | 21.41 | 05.20 | 21.23 | 04.41 | full moon |
| 27th | 23.03 | 05.58 | 22.48 | 05.15 | |
| 28th | — | 06.47 | 23.58 | 06.02 | |
| 29th | 00.13 | 07.50 | — | 07.05 | |
| 30th | 01.06 | 09.04 | 00.50 | 08.20 | |
| 31st | 01.44 | 10.22 | 01.26 | 09.40 | |

Where moonset times are before moonrise times, this is the setting of the previous night's moon.

# THE SKY

## At night

**4th:** Close approach of Saturn and the moon, rising at 03.30 in the southeast and visible until lost in the dawn at around 05.00 at an altitude of 10 degrees.

**15th:** Close approach of dim Mars and the moon, visible in the dusk from around 21.30 in the west at an altitude of 30 degrees, until setting at 00.30 on the 16th in the northwest.

**31st:** Close approach of Saturn and the moon, rising at 01.30 in the southeast and visible until lost in the dawn at around 04.30, at an altitude of 17 degrees.

## By day

**21st:** At solar midday (approximately 13.00 BST/IST) the sun reaches an altitude of 59 degrees at Lee-on-the-Solent in Hampshire and 52 degrees at Lairg in Scotland.

**31st:** Earliest sunrise, St Michael's Mount (05.17) and Hopton-on-Sea (04.37).

**31st:** Latest sunset, St Michael's Mount (21.21) and Hopton-on-Sea (21.05).

**1st–31st:** Daylight increases by 1h 21m at St Michael's Mount and by 1h 30m at Hopton-on-Sea.

## Sunrise and set

| | St Michael's Mount | | Hopton-on-Sea | |
|---|---|---|---|---|
| | Rise | Set | Rise | Set |
| 1st | 05.57 | 20.41 | 05.21 | 20.20 |
| 2nd | 05.55 | 20.42 | 05.19 | 20.21 |
| 3rd | 05.54 | 20.44 | 05.17 | 20.23 |
| 4th | 05.52 | 20.45 | 05.15 | 20.25 |
| 5th | 05.50 | 20.47 | 05.13 | 20.26 |
| 6th | 05.49 | 20.48 | 05.12 | 20.28 |
| 7th | 05.47 | 20.50 | 05.10 | 20.30 |
| 8th | 05.45 | 20.51 | 05.08 | 20.31 |
| 9th | 05.44 | 20.53 | 05.06 | 20.33 |
| 10th | 05.42 | 20.54 | 05.04 | 20.35 |
| 11th | 05.41 | 20.56 | 05.03 | 20.36 |
| 12th | 05.39 | 20.57 | 05.01 | 20.38 |
| 13th | 05.38 | 20.59 | 04.59 | 20.40 |
| 14th | 05.36 | 21.00 | 04.58 | 20.41 |
| 15th | 05.35 | 21.02 | 04.56 | 20.43 |
| 16th | 05.34 | 21.03 | 04.55 | 20.44 |
| 17th | 05.32 | 21.04 | 04.53 | 20.46 |
| 18th | 05.31 | 21.06 | 04.52 | 20.47 |
| 19th | 05.30 | 21.07 | 04.50 | 20.49 |
| 20th | 05.28 | 21.08 | 04.49 | 20.50 |
| 21st | 05.27 | 21.10 | 04.48 | 20.52 |
| 22nd | 05.26 | 21.11 | 04.46 | 20.53 |
| 23rd | 05.25 | 21.12 | 04.45 | 20.55 |
| 24th | 05.24 | 21.14 | 04.44 | 20.56 |
| 25th | 05.23 | 21.15 | 04.43 | 20.57 |
| 26th | 05.22 | 21.16 | 04.42 | 20.59 |
| 27th | 05.21 | 21.17 | 04.40 | 21.00 |
| 28th | 05.20 | 21.18 | 04.39 | 21.01 |
| 29th | 05.19 | 21.19 | 04.38 | 21.03 |
| 30th | 05.18 | 21.20 | 04.37 | 21.04 |
| 31st | 05.17 | 21.21 | 04.36 | 21.05 |

M

# THE SEA

### Average sea temperature

| | |
|---|---|
| Orkney: | 9.2°C |
| South Shields: | 9.9°C |
| Carrickfergus: | 10°C |
| Lowestoft: | 10.6°C |
| Aberystwyth: | 10.7°C |
| Bantry: | 11.8°C |
| Cowes: | 11.4°C |
| Penzance: | 11.8°C |

### Spring and neap tides

The spring tides are the most extreme tides of the month, with the highest rises and falls, and the neap tides are the least extreme, with the smallest. Exact timings vary around the coast, but expect them around the following dates:

**Spring tides:** 12th–13th and 27th–29th

**Neap tides:** 5th–6th and 20th–21st

In the tide timetable opposite, spring tides are shown with an asterisk.

## May tide timetable for Dover

For guidance on how to convert this for your local area, see page 8.

|  | High water | | Low water | |
|---|---|---|---|---|
|  | Morning | Afternoon | Morning | Afternoon |
| 1st | 02.30 | 14.54 | 10.02 | 22.20 |
| 2nd | 03.21 | 15.49 | 10.46 | 23.08 |
| 3rd | 04.21 | 16.50 | 11.38 | — |
| 4th | 05.29 | 18.00 | 00.09 | 12.46 |
| 5th | 06.57 | 19.25 | 01.26 | 14.06 |
| 6th | 08.41 | 20.50 | 02.49 | 15.24 |
| 7th | 09.43 | 21.47 | 04.07 | 16.33 |
| 8th | 10.27 | 22.32 | 05.09 | 17.28 |
| 9th | 11.03 | 23.11 | 05.58 | 18.12 |
| 10th | 11.35 | 23.47 | 06.38 | 18.48 |
| 11th | — | 12.07 | 07.10 | 19.19 |
| 12th | 00.20 | 12.38 | 07.36 | 19.44 * |
| 13th | 00.51 | 13.07 | 08.01 | 20.11 * |
| 14th | 01.16 | 13.33 | 08.26 | 20.39 |
| 15th | 01.37 | 13.54 | 08.55 | 21.11 |
| 16th | 02.01 | 14.21 | 09.27 | 21.45 |
| 17th | 02.33 | 14.58 | 10.01 | 22.22 |
| 18th | 03.16 | 15.48 | 10.41 | 23.08 |
| 19th | 04.14 | 17.00 | 11.31 | — |
| 20th | 05.56 | 18.33 | 00.09 | 12.41 |
| 21st | 07.21 | 19.45 | 01.36 | 14.16 |
| 22nd | 08.23 | 20.44 | 02.52 | 15.25 |
| 23rd | 09.17 | 21.36 | 03.53 | 16.23 |
| 24th | 10.04 | 22.23 | 04.51 | 17.18 |
| 25th | 10.50 | 23.10 | 05.48 | 18.13 |
| 26th | 11.35 | 23.56 | 06.45 | 19.06 |
| 27th | — | 12.20 | 07.37 | 19.55 * |
| 28th | 00.43 | 13.07 | 08.25 | 20.42 * |
| 29th | 01.30 | 13.55 | 09.10 | 21.28 * |
| 30th | 02.20 | 14.45 | 09.55 | 22.16 |
| 31st | 03.13 | 15.37 | 10.41 | 23.06 |

M

# A SEA SHANTY FOR MAY

### No More I'll Go to Sea

In this sea shanty, our sailor sets off for sea on a fine day in the month of May, perhaps for the last time (though this could have been a perennial cry…).

This may be a 'forebitter' or 'fo'c's'le' song, sung during the sailors' leisure time in the forecastle, their living quarters in the bow of the ship.

It was one fine day in the month of May and I was out-ward bound,

hadn't any tin to buy me gin, so I walked the streets all round. M

coat was out at the el-bows and I was sore in need, so I shipped as a jol-

sai-lor boy on board the An-gle - sea. No more I'll go to sea

cross the Wes - tern Oc - ean, a - hau - lin' and a - pul - lin', I

ne-ver will a - gain. No more I'll go to sea, a - cross the West-

Oc-ean. For ev - er-more I'll stay a-shore and go to sea no more!

No more at the cry aloft I fly,
With a grease-pot in my hand.
No more I'll reef, no more I'll furl,
Nor the brightwork scrape with sand.
No more I'll shout 'All's well, sir!'
For it is no more my trade,
And I'll go ashore for evermore
From on board the Anglesea.
*No more I'll go to sea*
*Across the Western Ocean,*
*A-hauling and a-pullin',*
*I never will again.*
*No more I'll go to sea*
*Across the Western Ocean.*
*For evermore I'll stay ashore*
*And go to sea no more!*

No more I'll pull on the lee-fore-brace
Nor by royal halyards stand,
I'll never sail again the raging main,
But I'll find me a wife on land.
I'll stay at home in comfort
No more my back will break
For I'll go ashore for evermore
From on board the Anglesea.
*No more…*

EUROPE

AFRICA

NORTH MIGRATION APRIL/MAY

SOUTH MIGRATION JUL/AUG

WINTER

A MAP OF
SWIFT MIGRATION

After a map by the British Trust for Ornithology, used with their permission

# MIGRATION OF THE MONTH

### Swift migration

For many of us the most joyful and visible migration of the year is that of the swifts. Their otherworldly elfin cries are the sound of the summer over many cities and towns. Swifts seem to thrive in the suburbs, creating screeching parties that build in number through the summer and swoop up and down our streets, all drama and acrobatics. Their cries are synonymous with hot pavements and the distant tinkling of ice cream vans.

Swifts spend almost their entire lives on the wing, feeding on flying insects, drinking, mating and even sleeping as they fly. They only ever stop to breed, and they choose to do that in the eaves of older houses and in the nest boxes on our streets, staying just a few months before setting off again on their epic trek south by the end of July. Keep your eyes and ears open: within the first few days of the month, you should have spotted your first few swooping birds.

They have spent most of the winter wheeling high above the mosaic of savannah and forest at the edge of the Congo Basin. They then took a jaunt across to Mozambique in eastern Africa and on to the Indian Ocean around December, presumably following the rains that produce some seasonal abundance of food. From here they headed back to the Congo until it was time to start their journey north. The first leg was right across to the Atlantic coast of Africa in early April, where they spent around two weeks fattening up to prepare for the final push. And then they were off.

Swifts fly fast and high: one individual tracked by the British Trust for Ornithology took just five days to travel 5,000km from West Africa to the United Kingdom, and others have been seen migrating at 5,700m in altitude. Up they come through Spain and France and finally swoop into our nesting boxes and eaves in late April and early May, just as the weather starts to warm. We fling our windows open and hear those cries – summer has arrived.

M

# THE GARDEN

### May garden meditation

There is no better month than May to take your five-minute meditation at dawn. Slip out and sit or stand quietly and you will be serenaded by the most beautiful chorus of song. The blackbirds, robins, wrens, thrushes and finches are defending territory and attracting mates, and dawn is when the air is at its stillest and so their song carries furthest, to reach the most beautiful birds, who may be hanging out a few streets away. Think about all of the bird activity that will be hidden in the hedges and trees of your neighbourhood over the coming month: birds choosing each other, nests being sculpted and lined, little speckled eggs being laid and nurtured, and then, just a couple of weeks later, chicks being born.

Look at the soft froth of new growth and hawthorn blossom that covers the trees and hedges now. Think about where that came from, how that potential was held deep inside the plant all winter. Note how young and vibrant it is: lime green, perfect and untouched. Observe how fleeting all of the flowers of May are – the lilacs, bluebells and blossom – and appreciate them in this, their brief moment.

## Jobs in the garden

- Plant out your tender vegetable plants – winter squash, courgettes, tomatoes – that were sown indoors earlier in spring. But beware late frosts, and be ready to protect with fleece if they are forecast.
- Make up hanging baskets and pots full of colourful tender bedding plants from the garden centre.
- Keep on top of weeds. Get in among your plants and do a good weed now, nipping the problem in the bud. Weeding is always easier after wet weather.

**M**

## How much to sow

It is tempting to sow whole packets of seeds and then be overwhelmed by seedlings or, later, great gluts of one type of vegetable. This guide will help you to sow roughly the amount you need for a family of four; adjust to suit your own circumstances and favourites. In every case, sow a small number more than suggested to allow for non-germination and seedling failure.

**Beetroot and carrots:** Repeat sow a 3-m row of each direct into the ground, covering the carrots with fleece.

**Mixed salad leaves:** Repeat broadcast sow a broad seed drill about 1m long for a cut-and-come-again crop.

**Radishes and spring onions:** Repeat direct sow a 1-m row of each.

**Florence fennel:** Under cover, sow ten more plants into pots.

**Borlotti beans:** Sow a 3-m row against a cane support frame.

**Brussels sprouts, sprouting broccoli and kale:** Sow into pots or straight into the ground. For Brussels sprouts and sprouting broccoli, sow six plants of two different varieties. For kale, sow four plants of two different varieties. If sowing direct, sow two seeds at each station, then remove the weaker seedling. Cover all with a brassica cage.

**Basil, indoors:** Sow a few seeds in each of eight pots.

# THE KITCHEN

### Romani recipe for May – Gypsy coffee

Dandelions are among the most abundant of the wild edible greens, with an earthy and just nicely bitter flavour. They can be found at the bases of hedgerows and in messy lawns and are best and mildest when young, though cooking does remove any excessive bitterness. You can cook them as you would nettle tips for Gypsy spinach (see page 68), adding a squeeze of lemon juice before serving.

But you can also make use of the roots, and the recipe for Gypsy coffee was apparently known to all old Romani people who had experienced hard times. Recipes based on the research of Romani and Traveller historian Robert Dawson.

Collect the roots, wash thoroughly, then roast and grind. Use the powder as a coffee substitute.

### In season

### In the hedgerows, woods and fields
**Wild greens:** Alexanders, beech leaves, bistort, burdock, chickweed, comfrey leaves, dandelion, fat hen, Good-King-Henry, hawthorn tips, hop tips, nettle tips, orache, rampion, salad burnet, sea beet, sorrel, tansy, watercress, wintercress, wood sorrel
**Wild herbs:** Cleavers, hairy bittercress, hedge garlic, lemon balm, wild marjoram, spearmint, sweet cicely, wild thyme, wild fennel
**Edible wild flowers:** Broom, borage, elderflower, chamomile, hawthorn, marigold, pansy, violet, wild rose
**Wild fruits:** Wild gooseberry

### From the seashore and rivers
**Fish and shellfish:** Herring, brown crab, lobster, sea trout, turbot, sardine, plaice, sea bass, mackerel, salmon
**Seaweeds:** Laver, pepper dulse, carragheen, egg wrack, sea lettuce, sugar kelp

### From the kitchen garden
**Vegetables:** Asparagus, broad beans, baby globe artichokes, peas, radishes, wild rocket, beetroot, cabbages, cauliflower, chard, endive, green garlic, lettuce, spring onions, spinach, spring greens, turnips, sorrel
**Herbs:** Chives and chive flowers, parsley, chervil

### From the farms
Cheddar strawberries (from the Cheddar Valley in Somerset), ewe's milk cheeses, Stinking Bishop, garlic yarg, Jersey Royal potatoes, Cornish and Ayrshire earlies, asparagus, spring lamb

### And traditional imports
Alphonso mangos

**M**

# RECIPES

### Coronation chicken sandwiches for Ascension

Ascension Day celebrates the Christian belief in Jesus' ascent to heaven, and it is traditional to picnic near wells (see page 115) or high up on a hilltop in order to fly a kite. Everything on this day is about the air, flying and birds, and so chicken – despite the fact that they are not the most impressive flyers – finds itself among the traditional foods of the day. A coronation chicken and watercress sandwich would make a retro but delicious addition to Ascension Day outdoor feasting.

**Makes 4**

**Ingredients**

*For the filling*

500g roast chicken

6 tablespoons mayonnaise

1 tablespoon mild curry powder

1 tablespoon mango chutney

1 tablespoon lime pickle, finely chopped

2 tablespoons sultanas

Salt and pepper

*For the sandwiches*

A couple of handfuls of watercress, washed

8 thick slices of freshly buttered bread

**Method**

Shred and chop the chicken and mix with the other filling ingredients. Store in the fridge and then make up into sandwiches with the watercress just before eating or setting off.

### Gooseberry and sweet cicely custard tarts

Gooseberry tarts were traditional foods for Whit Sunday fairs, but really just the fact that gooseberries are in their brief season is excuse enough to make these lovely tarts. They are particularly good if you can find a little aniseed-scented sweet cicely leaf to sprinkle into the custard, but make the tarts even if you don't have it, perhaps adding nutmeg instead.

### Makes 12

### Ingredients

36 gooseberries, washed, topped and tailed

2 tablespoons honey

500g all butter shortcrust pastry

7 egg yolks

90g caster sugar

700ml full fat milk

A few leaflets of sweet cicely, finely chopped, or ½ teaspoon of freshly ground nutmeg

### Method

Preheat the oven to 200°C/Gas Mark 6. Put the gooseberries into an oven dish and drizzle the honey over them, then bake for about 10 minutes, or until soft, collapsed and very slightly caramelised. Remove from the oven and set aside, leaving the oven on for baking the tart cases.

Take a muffin tray and lay a strip of baking parchment across each cup, to help you remove the tarts when they are cooked. On a floured surface, roll out the pastry to about 1–2mm thickness. Cut out 12 rounds, each 11cm across, and put them into the cups of the muffin tray, pushing them down into the bottom edges. Make a small rice-filled parchment pouch for each and drop it into the base to stop the pastry from puffing up. Bake for 10 minutes, then remove the pouch and bake for a further 5 minutes.

Meanwhile, to make the custard, beat the egg yolks and sugar together and then stir in the milk and tip all into a saucepan. Stir continually with a wooden spoon over a low heat until the mixture starts to thicken and you can draw a clean line through the custard coating the back of the spoon. Remove from the heat and stir in the sweet cicely or nutmeg.

Put 3 gooseberries into the base of each tart case and cover with the custard. Bake for 15 minutes and then turn the oven down to 180°C/Gas Mark 4 and bake for a further 10 minutes. Leave to cool completely before removing from the muffin tin.

# PILGRIMAGE OF THE MONTH

## Derbyshire's wells for Ascension Day

Wells have always been sites of pilgrimage and celebration, the places where pure, clean, life-giving water mysteriously appears from the ground being understandably venerated and invested with power and meaning. They have long been decorated with rags, ribbons and garlands of flowers by pilgrims seeking cures or saying prayers, but the people of Derbyshire take this tradition to elaborate and beautiful lengths with their well-dressing ceremonies. These occur throughout the county all summer but the main event is the wells at Tissington, which are always decorated on Ascension Day. Large boards are smeared with clay and then beautiful and colourful scenes and patterns are created using leaves and petals and the boards are erected around the wells.

Ascension Day, which falls 40 days after Easter Day, is this year on Thursday, 13th May, and marks the day upon which Christians believe that Jesus ascended to heaven. This image, of Jesus rising up into the air, has led the day to be traditionally associated with all things to do with the sky: with birds, clouds and rain, and in turn with wells and their water – water that falls on this day is believed to have special properties. It was traditional to visit wells on Ascension Day to bathe and cure ailments, as well as to picnic and celebrate, and water would be bottled and taken home for its healing qualities.

There is a theory that the particular lauding of the Tissington wells stems from the time of the Black Death of 1348–9, when the local village of Eyam was decimated by the plague but Tissington remained untouched, which became attributed to the purity of Tissington's water. The current form of the well dressing, however, only arose in Victorian times, as folk traditions were widely revived and reshaped. It has undergone several slumps and revivals but is currently enjoying a great flowering, with over a hundred villages around Derbyshire decorating their wells through late spring and summer.

M

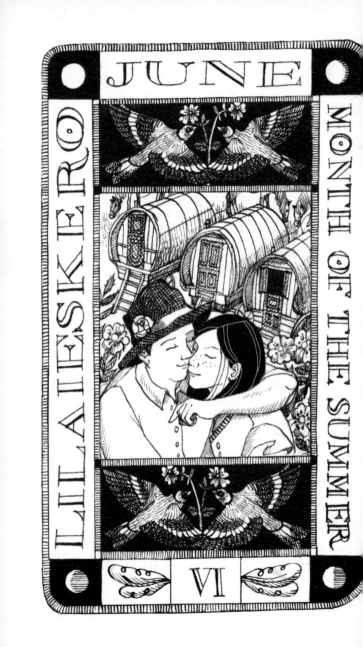

# June

 Start of meteorological summer

 Start of Pride Month

 Start of Gypsy, Roma and Traveller History Month

 Corpus Christi (Christian)

 3rd–8th: Appleby Horse Fair, Cumbria – Gypsy, Romani and Traveller gathering

 June bank holiday, Republic of Ireland

 The Queen's official birthday

 Father's Day

 Summer solstice – start of astronomical summer

 Midsummer/Midsummer's Day/Litha (pagan/neopagan/traditional)

World Humanist Day

Traditional English midsummer, combined with the Feast of St John the Baptist

# ROMANI NAME FOR THE MONTH

### Lilaieskero – month of the summer

Summer is here and the weather is suddenly gentle and easy. Appropriately, the Romani name for June means 'month of the summer'. In June many Romani families would have taken (and still do take) time out to visit the largest horse fair of the year, Appleby Fair, to dress up in their best, trade horses and meet friends and relations. But there was also work to be done. Each family would traditionally have an annual route that would take them around a number of different farmers with whom they had built up a relationship over the years. The Romani would undertake the seasonal jobs that needed a large workforce for a short amount of time.

Romani activist Maggie Smith-Bendell in her book *Our Forgotten Years* writes of how her family would always return to the same farmer at the end of May to pick peas and broad beans in June. They would travel along lanes draped with dog roses and punctuated by foxgloves, pull into the farmer's field and set up camp alongside a little stream. Gradually other travelling families that they may not have seen since the previous year would arrive and set up camp, too, and a joyful reunion take place. Once the farmer deemed the peas ripe, it was all hands to work, including the children, and as soon as the peas were picked it was on to the broad bean fields. Altogether this meant several weeks of hard work, good money and a safe and secure place to park your wagon among other travelling families. The atmosphere was lively with singing around the cooking fires as the sun went down in the warm midsummer evenings, and all the peas you could eat. 'Lilai' appears in lots of 'summer' words (such as *lilaieski rat* – Midsummer Eve; *lilaiesko cheriklo* – swallow) but it also means 'season', and *lilaieski rat lilaiesko lil* means 'almanac'.

# THE MOON

## Moon phases

3rd quarter – 2nd June, 08.24

New moon – 10th June, 11.53

1st quarter – 18th June, 04.54

Full moon – 24th June, 19.40

## Gardening by the moon

**Full moon to 3rd quarter: 1st–2nd and 24th–30th.** Harvest crops for immediate eating. Harvest fruit.

**3rd quarter to new moon: 2nd–10th.** Prune. Harvest for storage. Fertilise and mulch the soil.

**New moon to 1st quarter: 10th–18th.** Sow crops that develop below ground. Dig the soil.

**1st quarter to full moon: 18th–24th.** Sow crops that develop above ground. Plant seedlings and young plants.

## Moon sign – Gemini

Astrologers believe that the new moon is a time to make plans and focus on your dreams and hopes for the period ahead, and that each new moon has a particular energy, depending on which zodiacal sign it is in. The new moon on the 10th will be in Gemini, which is said to rule communication, meaning this is a good time for making connections, socialising and conveying ideas.

### Navigating by the stars, sun and moon

#### Make a sun or moon compass

This method will allow you to create a rough compass that will give you a good sense of your direction, as long as the sun is shining or the moon is bright. Find an area of flat ground and push a straight stick (roughly 60cm long) into it, or prop it upright with rocks and pebbles if the ground is too hard. Place a pebble at the end of the shadow and mark it with a W. Wait around 20 minutes and the shadow will move, as both the sun and moon move from east to west across the sky. Take a second pebble and place it at the end of the shadow and mark it with an E. Draw a straight line or lay a straight stick between the two points, then set another straight line or stick perpendicular to it. Place pebbles at each end and mark them N and S, remembering that the order, going clockwise is N – E – S – W: 'Never Eat Shredded Wheat'.

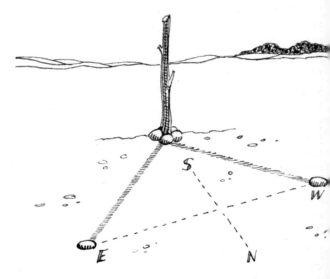

## Moon rise and set

| | St Michael's Mount | | Hopton-on-Sea | | |
|------|------|------|------|------|------|
| | Rise | Set | Rise | Set | |
| 1st | 02.12 | 11.39 | 01.52 | 11.00 | |
| 2nd | 02.34 | 12.53 | 02.11 | 12.17 | 3rd quarter |
| 3rd | 02.52 | 14.04 | 02.26 | 13.31 | |
| 4th | 03.08 | 15.12 | 02.40 | 14.42 | |
| 5th | 03.22 | 16.19 | 02.52 | 15.51 | |
| 6th | 03.37 | 17.26 | 03.05 | 17.01 | |
| 7th | 03.53 | 18.34 | 03.19 | 18.11 | |
| 8th | 04.12 | 19.42 | 03.35 | 19.21 | |
| 9th | 04.35 | 20.49 | 03.55 | 20.31 | |
| 10th | 05.04 | 21.53 | 04.22 | 21.37 | new moon |
| 11th | 05.41 | 22.51 | 04.57 | 22.36 | |
| 12th | 06.28 | 23.40 | 05.43 | 23.26 | |
| 13th | 07.26 | — | 06.41 | — | |
| 14th | 08.32 | 00.20 | 07.49 | 00.04 | |
| 15th | 09.44 | 00.52 | 09.03 | 00.34 | |
| 16th | 10.58 | 01.18 | 10.21 | 00.56 | |
| 17th | 12.15 | 01.39 | 11.40 | 01.15 | |
| 18th | 13.32 | 01.57 | 13.00 | 01.31 | 1st quarter |
| 19th | 14.52 | 02.15 | 14.23 | 01.46 | |
| 20th | 16.14 | 02.33 | 15.48 | 02.01 | |
| 21st | 17.40 | 02.53 | 17.17 | 02.19 | |
| 22nd | 19.08 | 03.18 | 18.48 | 02.40 | |
| 23rd | 20.34 | 03.49 | 20.17 | 03.08 | |
| 24th | 21.51 | 04.31 | 21.36 | 03.47 | full moon |
| 25th | 22.53 | 05.28 | 22.38 | 04.42 | |
| 26th | 22.39 | 06.38 | 23.22 | 05.53 | |
| 27th | — | 07.56 | 23.53 | 07.14 | |
| 28th | 00.12 | 09.17 | — | 08.37 | |
| 29th | 00.37 | 10.34 | 00.15 | 09.58 | |
| 30th | 00.57 | 11.48 | 00.32 | 11.14 | |

Where moonset times are before moonrise times, this is the setting of the previous night's moon.

# THE SKY

## At night

**1st:** Close approach of Jupiter and the moon, rising at 02.00 in the southeast and visible until lost in the dawn at about 04.00 in the southeast at an altitude of 17 degrees.

**12th:** Close approach of Venus and the moon, visible in the dusk from about 21.30 in the northwest, at an altitude of 9 degrees, until setting at 22.30 in the northwest.

**13th:** Close approach of a dim Mars and the moon, visible in the dusk from 22.00 in the west–northwest, at an altitude of 15 degrees, until setting at 00.30 in the northwest.

**27th:** Close approach of Saturn and the moon, rising at 00.30 in the southeast, and visible until lost in the dawn at about 04.00 in the south, at an altitude of 16 degrees.

**29th:** Close approach of Jupiter and the moon, rising at 00.30 in the southeast, and visible until lost in the dawn at around 04.00 in the south at an altitude of 23 degrees.

## By day

**10th:** Partial eclipse of the sun, beginning at 10.04. It will be at its maximum at 11.09 and will end at 12.19.

**21st:** The summer solstice falls at 03.32, when the North Pole is at its maximum tilt towards the sun.

**17th:** Earliest sunrise, St Michael's Mount (05.11), Hopton-on-Sea (04.29).

**24th/25th:** Latest sunset, Hopton-on-Sea (24th, 21.20), St Michael's Mount (25th, 21.35).

**1st–21st:** Daylight increases by oh 18m at St Michael's Mount and by oh 20m at Hopton-on-Sea.

**21st–30th:** Daylight decreases by oh 3m at St Michael's Mount and by oh 5m at Hopton-on-Sea.

## Sunrise and set

| | *St Michael's Mount* | | *Hopton-on-Sea* | |
|---|---|---|---|---|
| | Rise | Set | Rise | Set |
| 1st | 05.17 | 21.23 | 04.36 | 21.06 |
| 2nd | 05.16 | 21.24 | 04.35 | 21.07 |
| 3rd | 05.15 | 21.24 | 04.34 | 21.08 |
| 4th | 05.15 | 21.25 | 04.33 | 21.09 |
| 5th | 05.14 | 21.26 | 04.33 | 21.10 |
| 6th | 05.14 | 21.27 | 04.32 | 21.11 |
| 7th | 05.13 | 21.28 | 04.32 | 21.12 |
| 8th | 05.13 | 21.29 | 04.31 | 21.13 |
| 9th | 05.12 | 21.29 | 04.31 | 21.14 |
| 10th | 05.12 | 21.30 | 04.30 | 21.14 |
| 11th | 05.12 | 21.31 | 04.30 | 21.15 |
| 12th | 05.11 | 21.31 | 04.30 | 21.16 |
| 13th | 05.11 | 21.32 | 04.29 | 21.16 |
| 14th | 05.11 | 21.33 | 04.29 | 21.17 |
| 15th | 05.11 | 21.33 | 04.29 | 21.18 |
| 16th | 05.11 | 21.33 | 04.29 | 21.18 |
| 17th | 05.11 | 21.34 | 04.29 | 21.18 |
| 18th | 05.11 | 21.34 | 04.29 | 21.19 |
| 19th | 05.11 | 21.35 | 04.29 | 21.19 |
| 20th | 05.11 | 21.35 | 04.29 | 21.19 |
| 21st | 05.12 | 21.35 | 04.29 | 21.20 |
| 22nd | 05.12 | 21.35 | 04.30 | 21.20 |
| 23rd | 05.12 | 21.35 | 04.30 | 21.20 |
| 24th | 05.12 | 21.35 | 04.30 | 21.20 |
| 25th | 05.13 | 21.35 | 04.31 | 21.20 |
| 26th | 05.13 | 21.35 | 04.31 | 21.20 |
| 27th | 05.14 | 21.35 | 04.32 | 21.20 |
| 28th | 05.14 | 21.35 | 04.32 | 21.19 |
| 29th | 05.15 | 21.35 | 04.33 | 21.19 |
| 30th | 05.15 | 21.35 | 04.33 | 21.19 |

J

# THE SEA

## Average sea temperature

| | |
|---|---:|
| Orkney: | 11.2°C |
| South Shields: | 12.7°C |
| Carrickfergus: | 11.8°C |
| Lowestoft: | 13.4°C |
| Aberystwyth: | 12.7°C |
| Bantry: | 13.3°C |
| Cowes: | 13.4°C |
| Penzance: | 14°C |

## Spring and neap tides

The spring tides are the most extreme tides of the month, with the highest rises and falls, and the neap tides are the least extreme, with the smallest. Exact timings vary around the coast, but expect them around the following dates:

**Spring tides:** 10th–11th and 25th–26th

**Neap tides:** 3rd–4th and 19th–20th

In the tide timetable opposite, spring tides are shown with an asterisk.

## June tide timetable for Dover

For guidance on how to convert this for your local area, see page 8.

|  | *High water* | | *Low water* | |
|---|---|---|---|---|
|  | Morning | Afternoon | Morning | Afternoon |
| 1st | 04.09 | 16.32 | 11.31 | — |
| 2nd | 05.10 | 17.31 | 00.02 | 12.29 |
| 3rd | 06.19 | 18.38 | 01.05 | 13.34 |
| 4th | 07.43 | 19.54 | 02.11 | 14.38 |
| 5th | 08.51 | 21.00 | 03.14 | 15.38 |
| 6th | 09.42 | 21.52 | 04.12 | 16.34 |
| 7th | 10.23 | 22.36 | 05.04 | 17.23 |
| 8th | 11.01 | 23.15 | 05.48 | 18.05 |
| 9th | 11.37 | 23.51 | 06.25 | 18.41 |
| 10th | — | 12.11 | 06.59 | 19.14 * |
| 11th | 00.23 | 12.43 | 07.32 | 19.48 * |
| 12th | 00.53 | 13.13 | 08.06 | 20.23 |
| 13th | 01.22 | 13.43 | 08.40 | 20.58 |
| 14th | 01.52 | 14.15 | 09.15 | 21.36 |
| 15th | 02.28 | 14.54 | 09.52 | 22.15 |
| 16th | 03.10 | 15.41 | 10.31 | 23.00 |
| 17th | 04.03 | 16.38 | 11.18 | 23.53 |
| 18th | 05.09 | 17.44 | — | 12.15 |
| 19th | 06.27 | 18.55 | 00.59 | 13.27 |
| 20th | 07.40 | 20.02 | 02.09 | 14.39 |
| 21st | 08.42 | 21.03 | 03.14 | 15.44 |
| 22nd | 09.37 | 21.59 | 04.16 | 16.46 |
| 23rd | 10.31 | 22.53 | 05.19 | 17.48 |
| 24th | 11.22 | 23.46 | 06.23 | 18.47 |
| 25th | — | 12.12 | 07.22 | 19.43 * |
| 26th | 00.36 | 13.00 | 08.16 | 20.36 * |
| 27th | 01.25 | 13.47 | 09.05 | 21.25 |
| 28th | 02.14 | 14.33 | 09.50 | 22.12 |
| 29th | 03.02 | 15.20 | 10.33 | 22.57 |
| 30th | 03.51 | 16.08 | 11.15 | 23.42 |

J

# A SEA SHANTY FOR JUNE

## Blow Ye Winds

An unusually mystical subject for a sea shanty – most are concerned with far more practical and earthy subjects such as money, women and work – but to be fair it does approach mermaids and mermen in a characteristically robust fashion. 'Blow Ye Winds' is a capstan shanty, used for hauling up the anchor (see page 42).

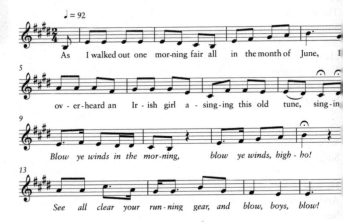

As I walked out one mor-ning fair all in the month of June, I
ov-er-heard an Ir-ish girl a - sing-ing this old tune, sing-in
Blow ye winds in the mor-ning, blow ye winds, high - ho!
See all clear your run-ning gear, and blow, boys, blow!

Our ship she lay at anchor with the men at work about
When 'neath the bow we heard a splash and then a lusty
  shout.
Singing, *Blow ye winds in the morning,*
*Blow ye winds, high-ho!*
*See all clear your running gear,*
*And blow, boys, blow!*

'Man overboard!' The lookout cried and forward we all ran,
There hanging to our larboard chains we saw a green merman.
Singing, *Blow ye winds...*

His hair was blue and eyes were green, his mouth as big as three,
The long green tail he sat on was still waving in the sea.
Singing, *Blow ye winds...*

He spoke to us as bold as brass 'A plea I have to bring:
You've dropped your anchor on my house and trapped my
  family in.'
Singing, *Blow ye winds...*

Our anchor we brought up at once and set his family free,
We asked him how he came to be a creature in the sea.
Singing, *Blow ye winds...*

He told us he fell overboard while sailing in a gale
And down below where seaweeds grow, he met a girl with a tail.
Singing, *Blow ye winds...*

She saved his life, became his wife, and his legs changed instantly
And now he lives in comfort at the bottom of the sea.
Singing, *Blow ye winds...*

ARCTIC CIRCLE

EUROPE

TROPIC OF CANCER

AFRICA

· A MAP OF ·
PAINTED LADY
BUTTERFLY MIGRATION

# MIGRATION OF THE MONTH

**Painted lady butterflies**

High above our heads, great clouds of painted lady butterflies are arriving on summer breezes. Or more accurately, they are just now passing through, because the painted lady has no real destination: its life is a constant journey.

This delicate butterfly with its orange and dark brown patterned, paper-thin wings has a monumental migration. The population we see in British and Irish gardens each year travels annually from tropical Africa to the Arctic and back again, the longest migration of any butterfly. However, no single individual will complete the entire migration. It takes up to six successive generations to make the entire 12,000-km round trip each year, guided by some innate drive and the position of the sun: no parent has ever taught a painted lady butterfly the route. It was once thought that the butterflies died when they reached the north, but we now know that the return journey south is done at such altitude that no one had seen them travel.

What the painted lady is searching for in this endlessly restless life is perfect breeding conditions. They breed all year round, continually adjusting their latitude rather than ever changing their modus operandi to fit in with the seasons. The painted lady chases summer up and down the northern hemisphere, hitching a ride on favourable winds, and trying its luck in every varying climate.

So when they arrive here this month, it is simply because we now have the good stuff: warmth but not too much, plenty of rain and lush growth. The male perches somewhere that a female is likely to pass by, and a courtship dance plays out, with up to eight butterflies fluttering in circles around each other. The lucky pair land and mate back to back, and the female lays her eggs on a particularly promising bit of greenery – a thistle or aster out of choice – before moving on to try again elsewhere, and again and again. Her eggs will soon hatch into caterpillars which will fatten up and pupate and then pick up the baton for their own leg of this endless migration.

# THE GARDEN

### June garden meditation

June is the month for a garden meditation at dusk, as the magical boundary between afternoon and night now stretches out luxuriously, over hours. Go barefoot into the garden and stand or take a seat. Feel how the earth beneath your toes has warmed. Think about the texture of what you feel, be it sun-warmed stone, or soft grass or even squelchy mud. What does the sensation tell you about the year's weather so far? We are at the moment when the northern hemisphere is tilted as far as it will go towards the sun. Close your eyes and feel the sun on your face, or open them and watch the sunset and think about the fact that this is the tipping point of the year, the pinnacle. Let your mind run over the first six months of the year in your garden, how it has grown, swollen and blossomed from the dark twiggy days of the beginning of the year until now, when it is full and beautiful and flower-filled. Now think ahead to the next six months, how it will start to ripen as the days shorten, and then pull back in on itself, before closing back down. Don't be sad, there is plenty of summer left to go, but embrace this moment for what it is. Allow it to encourage you to enjoy the summer in your garden to the full, because it doesn't last for ever, and there's nothing like it.

## Jobs in the garden

- Fruit trees will shed fruits this month in the 'June drop' to allow them to properly ripen a few, but they always keep too many fruits. Thin them out further.
- Deadhead roses as they go over. Feed the roses and all flowering plants with an organic tomato fertiliser, which helps to encourage more flowers.
- Keep a good compost heap. Add as much dry material as wet green material, shredded into small pieces. Turn it regularly and water it if it gets dry.

## How much to sow

It is tempting to sow whole packets of seeds and then be overwhelmed by seedlings or, later, great gluts of one type of vegetable. This guide will help you to sow roughly the amount you need for a family of four; adjust to suit your own circumstances and favourites. In every case, sow a small number more than suggested to allow for non-germination and seedling failure. Sowing is slowing down now, but there are still a few things you can sow to keep the season going later on.

**Courgettes:** In pots or straight into the ground, sow three more plants each of three different varieties.

**Kale and purple sprouting broccoli:** If you didn't sow your brassicas last month, you can still sow kale and purple sprouting broccoli. See May for numbers.

**Winter/maincrop carrots and beetroot:** Sow a 3-m row of each for winter cropping.

**Mixed salad leaves:** Broadcast sow 1m again.

**Florence fennel:** Sow ten plants, direct.

**Sweetcorn:** In early June there is still just time to sow sweetcorn direct. Sow a 'block' of 20 plants spaced about 30cm apart each way.

**Basil:** Sow in eight pots with a few seeds in each, or direct into the ground if warm.

# THE KITCHEN

### Romani recipe for June – Marrikli – Gypsy cake

This is a 'cake' cooked on a griddle or in a frying pan on the stove top or over a fire – much like Welsh cakes are and scones used to be. Recipe based on the research of Romani and Traveller historian Robert Dawson.

Rub 125g of lard or butter into 450g self-raising flour. Add 125g sultanas or currants and enough water to form a stiff dough. Knead lightly and roll out to 5mm thick on a floured surface. Grease a large frying pan so that it is just shiny, then place the cake in the pan and cook over a low heat, turning frequently. Test with a skewer to see if it is cooked. Serve with butter.

### In season

### In the hedgerows, woods and fields
**Wild herbs:** Cleavers, hairy bittercress, hedge garlic, lemon balm, wild marjoram, pineapple weed, spearmint, sweet cicely, watercress, water mint, wild thyme, wild fennel
**Edible wild flowers:** Broom, borage, elderflower, chamomile, hawthorn, honeysuckle, lime, marigold, meadowsweet, nasturtium, pansy, red clover, wild rose
**Wild fruits:** Wild strawberries, wild gooseberries
**Game:** Wood pigeon

## From the seashore and rivers
**Fish and shellfish:** Mackerel, sea trout, brown crab, herring, lobster, turbot, sardines, salmon
**Seaweeds:** Laver, pepper dulse, carragheen, egg wrack, sea lettuce, sugar kelp

## From the kitchen garden
**Vegetables:** Globe artichokes, rhubarb, asparagus, calabrese, carrots, courgettes, cucumber, broad beans, cauliflower, chard, endive, lettuce, spring greens, spring onions, new potatoes, radishes, wild rocket, spinach, beetroot, garlic, peas, turnips
**Fruits:** Gooseberries, strawberries, blackcurrants, cherries, loganberries, raspberries, redcurrants
**Herbs:** Chives, basil, mint, dill, marjoram, thyme, oregano

## From the farms
Asparagus, Cheddar strawberries (see page 111), Ayrshire and Cornish new potatoes, fresh goat's milk cheese, Stinking Bishop, ewe's curd, ricotta, new season lamb

## And traditional imports
Alphonso mangos, apricots, peaches, nectarines and cherries

# RECIPES

### Malfatti with broad beans and bacon

Malfatti are beautiful, light, little ricotta and spinach dumplings, and they turn a simple plate of broad beans and bacon into a treat meal.

**Serves 4**

**Ingredients**

*For the malfatti*

500g spinach

250g ricotta

2 eggs, beaten

½ teaspoon grated nutmeg

125g grated Parmesan cheese, plus extra slivers to top

250g plain flour

*For the broad beans and bacon*

1kg broad beans, out of their pods

150g butter

500g bacon

Salt and pepper

## Method

For the malfatti, wash the spinach, drain, put into a pan over heat with no other other liquid, and cover with a lid – it will collapse completely. Drain, cool and chop it roughly, squeeze out the excess liquid and then chop again. Put it in a large bowl and add the ricotta, eggs, nutmeg, grated Parmesan, 100g of the flour, and salt and pepper to taste. Mix well. Tip the rest of the flour onto a plate, and scoop out balls of the mixture, rolling them in the flour.

Bring a large pan of well salted water to the boil, and drop the dumplings in one by one. They will float to the surface when they are cooked. Fish them out with a slotted spoon, and keep them warm until ready to serve.

Cook the broad beans in boiling water for 3–4 minutes, drain and tip into a bowl of cold water, then spend a few minutes 'double podding', or slipping them out of their shells. Set aside.

Heat a knob of the butter in a frying pan, cut the bacon into bite-sized pieces, and fry until it starts to crisp up. Tip in the broad beans and cook for a few minutes, until some turn a little crispy, then add the rest of the butter and let it melt. Add the malfatti and stir carefully so that they are coated in the bacon-flavoured butter, then serve in individual bowls with slivers of Parmesan on top.

J

### Warm strawberries with honey, thyme and rose ricotta

June strawberries generally don't need much help, but if
you have a glut of them and want to try something a little
different, or if you come across a rare batch of underripe June
strawberries, try this. Warming them brings out the juices, and
the smell is gorgeous – intensely fruity and lightly spicy.

| Serves 4 |
| --- |
| **Ingredients** |
| 400g strawberries, hulled and quartered |
| Juice of half a lemon |
| ½ tablespoon icing sugar |
| 250g ricotta |
| 1 tablespoon runny honey |
| Leaves from sprig of fresh thyme |
| 1 teaspoon rosewater |

#### Method

Put the strawberries in a saucepan over a low heat with the lemon
juice and icing sugar. As they warm up, the juice will be released
so that they are gently poaching in it, but if they are a little dry
at first you can add more lemon juice to get them started. Once
the juice is flowing, bring to a gentle simmer for 1–2 minutes,
stirring, then remove from the heat and set aside.

In a bowl mix the ricotta with the honey, thyme and
rosewater. Divide between 4 bowls and spoon the strawberries
and their juices over the top.

# PILGRIMAGE OF THE MONTH

### Appleby Horse Fair

In the first week of June, the small town of Appleby in Cumbria fills with horses. Outside every shop, hotel and bar, horses are tethered. They splash in the river and trot along the lanes. Appleby Horse Fair holds a special importance in the British and Irish calendar, albeit one of which the vast majority of us are unaware. It is the largest event in the Gypsy, Romani and Traveller year, drawing around ten thousand members of the travelling community – British Romanichal, Irish Travellers, Scottish Gypsies and Travellers, and Kale (Welsh Romanies) from across Britain and Ireland, bringing with them a thousand caravans and several hundred horse-drawn carriages. The Appleby Horse Fair is the largest horse fair in the world and the biggest traditional Gypsy fair in Europe.

Since the late 18th century, it has been held just outside the town on what was once called Gallows Hill and is now called Fair Hill. Last year's cancellation was only the second time the fair had not gone ahead in 250 years.

The main event is the washing of horses in the Sands, an area of shallows in the River Eden near Appleby town centre, after which they are 'flashed', or raced up and down nearby Long Marton Road, known among the Gypsies as Flashing Lane. The event lasts from the first Thursday in June to the following Tuesday (visitors are encouraged over the weekend), during which time palms are read and fortunes told, music played and horses traded. Travellers' wares are bought and sold, including Waterford crystal, gold earrings and chains, fine clothing and harnesses and carts. But above all this is a social gathering, particularly for the young men and women, for whom marrying within the community is traditional. Many future marriages will be set into motion. The fair shores up traditions, and acts as a reminder of the importance of their history, and the strength of their community for this small, scattered and still much persecuted minority.

# July

- **10** Wimbledon Women's Final

- **11** Wimbledon Men's Final

- **11** Sea Sunday (Christian)

- **11** UEFA Euro 2020 final

- **12** Battle of the Boyne commemoration and bank holiday, Northern Ireland

- **15** St Swithin's Day (Christian, traditional)

- **18** Tisha B'Av Jewish day of mourning – begins at sunset the night before

- **19** 19th–23rd: Hajj – Muslim pilgrimage to Mecca

- **23** Birthday of Haile Selassie (Rastafarian)

- **23** Olympics opening ceremony, Japan

# ROMANI NAME FOR THE MONTH

## Kaseskero – month of the hay

From high summer through to autumn, all of the Romani names of the month refer to the big seasonal jobs that the Romani would have traditionally returned to year after year. This was the busy and lucrative time of year for Romani families, when they would try to earn enough to keep them going into winter. July's Kaseskero is the first of these and refers to haymaking. Farmers then, as now, grew fields of grasses and wild flowers and then turned them into dried hay to store, so that they would have a source of such stuff to feed their livestock over winter. This was and is an essential job in the farming year, and one requiring lots of manpower and muscle, too, making it the perfect job for the Romanies.

The farmer will wait for a spell of dry weather before giving the signal to start cutting the hay. The relationship of the word Kaseskero to the word for scythe – *kasarengi* – suggests that at the time that these names were widely used, this job was still done with a scythe, making it a slow and hugely labour-intensive job. The cut grass was left to dry out in the sun for a few hours, and then the workers returned to the field and used pitchforks and hay rakes to spread it out as much as possible, leaving it for a few hours more and then rolling it into rows in the evening. The next morning it was spread out again, turned and rolled, and so on for several days until it was dry enough to be formed into a haystack (a *kas*). As one section of field was drying, another would be being cut, and so this job might spread over several summer weeks, all dependent on how much the sun was shining. Once the job was done, the wagons would be hitched up to the well-rested horses and the Romanies would be off down the late-summer lanes – perhaps gathering handfuls of summer herbs and early berries as they went – to their next stopping place and their next big job.

# THE MOON

## Moon phases

3rd quarter – 1st July, 22.11

New moon – 10th July, 02.17

1st quarter – 17th July, 11.11

Full moon – 24th July, 03.37*

3rd quarter – 31st July, 14.16

## Gardening by the moon

**3rd quarter to new moon: 1st–10th.** Prune. Harvest for storage. Fertilise and mulch the soil.

**New moon to 1st quarter: 10th–17th.** Sow crops that develop below ground. Dig the soil.

**1st quarter to full moon: 17th–24th.** Sow crops that develop above ground. Plant seedlings and young plants.

**Full moon to 3rd quarter: 24th–31st.** Harvest crops for immediate eating. Harvest fruit.

## Moon sign – Cancer

Astrologers believe that the new moon is a time to make plans and focus on your dreams and hopes for the period ahead, and that each new moon has a particular energy, depending on which zodiacal sign it is in. The new moon on the 10th will be in Cancer, which is said to rule the home and family, making this a good time to nurture yourself and your family.

*This month the full moon falls in the early hours of the morning. To see the moon at its fullest within normal waking hours, view it the evening before the date given above.

## Navigating by the stars, sun and moon

### Use the Navigator's Triangle

This triangle of stars is actually an asterism, a particularly noticeable collection of stars – in this case Altair, Deneb and Vega – rather than a constellation. All belong to their own constellations (Aquila, Cygnus and Lyra, respectively), but they are so noticeable because they are among the brightest stars in the sky. This asterism is most commonly called the Summer Triangle because it is at its highest and most visible through June, July and August, but in the past it was referred to as the Navigator's Triangle, because of its use for pointing due south. As with all constellations, it will change orientation as it moves through the sky through the night, beginning with the 'fat' end of the triangle tipped across to the left. When this has swung up and the sharp end of the triangle points directly downwards, you are looking directly south. The Summer Triangle is also useful for a bit of in-sky navigation, as the Milky Way runs straight through it.

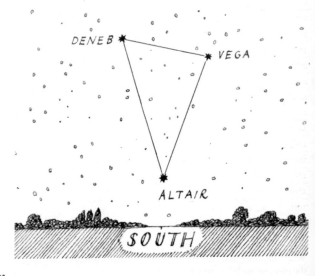

## Moon rise and set

| | St Michael's Mount | | Hopton-on-Sea | | |
|---|---|---|---|---|---|
| | Rise | Set | Rise | Set | |
| 1st | 01.14 | 12.59 | 00.47 | 12.28 | 3rd quarter |
| 2nd | 01.29 | 14.08 | 01.00 | 13.39 | |
| 3rd | 01.44 | 15.15 | 01.12 | 14.49 | |
| 4th | 02.00 | 16.23 | 01.26 | 15.59 | |
| 5th | 02.17 | 17.31 | 01.41 | 17.09 | |
| 6th | 02.39 | 18.38 | 02.00 | 18.20 | |
| 7th | 03.05 | 19.44 | 02.24 | 19.27 | |
| 8th | 03.40 | 20.44 | 02.56 | 20.29 | |
| 9th | 04.24 | 21.37 | 03.39 | 21.22 | |
| 10th | 05.18 | 22.21 | 04.33 | 22.05 | new moon |
| 11th | 06.23 | 22.55 | 05.39 | 22.37 | |
| 12th | 07.34 | 23.22 | 06.53 | 23.02 | |
| 13th | 08.49 | 23.45 | 08.10 | 23.22 | |
| 14th | 10.05 | — | 09.29 | 23.38 | |
| 15th | 11.21 | 00.04 | 10.48 | 23.53 | |
| 16th | 12.39 | 00.21 | 12.09 | — | |
| 17th | 13.58 | 00.39 | 13.31 | 00.08 | 1st quarter |
| 18th | 15.20 | 00.57 | 14.56 | 00.24 | |
| 19th | 16.44 | 01.19 | 16.23 | 00.42 | |
| 20th | 18.09 | 01.46 | 17.51 | 01.07 | |
| 21st | 19.28 | 02.22 | 19.13 | 01.40 | |
| 22nd | 20.36 | 03.11 | 20.22 | 02.26 | |
| 23rd | 21.29 | 04.14 | 21.14 | 03.29 | |
| 24th | 22.08 | 05.29 | 21.50 | 04.45 | full moon |
| 25th | 22.37 | 06.50 | 22.17 | 06.08 | |
| 26th | 22.59 | 08.10 | 22.36 | 07.32 | |
| 27th | 23.18 | 09.28 | 22.52 | 08.52 | |
| 28th | 23.34 | 10.41 | 23.05 | 10.09 | |
| 29th | 23.49 | 11.52 | 23.18 | 11.22 | |
| 30th | — | 13.01 | 23.31 | 12.34 | |
| 31st | 00.04 | 14.10 | 23.46 | 13.45 | 3rd quarter |

Where moonset times are before moonrise times, this is the setting of the previous night's moon.

# THE SKY

## At night

**12th:** Close approach of Venus and the moon, visible in the dusk from about 21.30 in the west at an altitude of 10 degrees, until setting at 22.30 in the northwest. Mars is also visible, with difficulty, close to Venus.

**24th–25th:** Close approach of Saturn and the moon, rising at 22.00 in the southeast, reaching a maximum altitude of 16 degrees in the south at 01.30 and becoming lost in the dawn at 04.30 on the 25th.

**25th–26th:** Close approach of Jupiter and the moon, rising at 22.30 in the southeast, reaching a maximum altitude of 23 degrees in the south at 03.00 and visible until lost in the dawn at an altitude of 20 degrees in the southwest.

## By day

**5th:** Aphelion. This is the moment in the year at which the earth is furthest from the sun in its elliptical orbit. At 23.27 the sun will be 152,100,527km away (compare with perihelion, on 2nd January).

**21st:** At solar midday (approximately 13.00 BST/IST) the sun reaches an altitude of 60 degrees at Lee-on-the-Solent in Hampshire and 52 degrees at Lairg in Scotland.

**1st:** Earliest sunrise, St Michael's Mount (05.16) and Hopton-on-Sea (04.34).

**1st:** Latest sunset, St Michael's Mount (21.34), latest sunset, Hopton-on-Sea, 29th (21.19).

**1st–31st:** Daylight decreases by 1h 2m at St Michael's Mount and by 1h 9m at Hopton-on-Sea.

**Sunrise and set**

| | St Michael's Mount | | Hopton-on-Sea | |
|---|---|---|---|---|
| | Rise | Set | Rise | Set |
| 1st | 05.16 | 21.34 | 04.34 | 21.19 |
| 2nd | 05.17 | 21.34 | 04.35 | 21.18 |
| 3rd | 05.17 | 21.34 | 04.36 | 21.18 |
| 4th | 05.18 | 21.33 | 04.36 | 21.17 |
| 5th | 05.19 | 21.33 | 04.37 | 21.17 |
| 6th | 05.20 | 21.32 | 04.38 | 21.16 |
| 7th | 05.21 | 21.32 | 04.39 | 21.15 |
| 8th | 05.21 | 21.31 | 04.40 | 21.15 |
| 9th | 05.22 | 21.30 | 04.41 | 21.14 |
| 10th | 05.23 | 21.30 | 04.42 | 21.13 |
| 11th | 05.24 | 21.29 | 04.43 | 21.12 |
| 12th | 05.25 | 21.28 | 04.44 | 21.11 |
| 13th | 05.26 | 21.27 | 04.46 | 21.10 |
| 14th | 05.27 | 21.26 | 04.47 | 21.09 |
| 15th | 05.29 | 21.26 | 04.48 | 21.08 |
| 16th | 05.30 | 21.25 | 04.49 | 21.07 |
| 17th | 05.31 | 21.24 | 04.51 | 21.06 |
| 18th | 05.32 | 21.23 | 04.52 | 21.05 |
| 19th | 05.33 | 21.21 | 04.53 | 21.04 |
| 20th | 05.34 | 21.20 | 04.55 | 21.02 |
| 21st | 05.36 | 21.19 | 04.56 | 21.01 |
| 22nd | 05.37 | 21.18 | 04.57 | 21.00 |
| 23rd | 05.38 | 21.17 | 04.59 | 20.58 |
| 24th | 05.40 | 21.15 | 05.00 | 20.57 |
| 25th | 05.41 | 21.14 | 05.02 | 20.55 |
| 26th | 05.42 | 21.13 | 05.03 | 20.54 |
| 27th | 05.44 | 21.11 | 05.05 | 20.52 |
| 28th | 05.45 | 21.10 | 05.06 | 20.51 |
| 29th | 05.46 | 21.09 | 05.08 | 20.49 |
| 30th | 05.48 | 21.07 | 05.09 | 20.48 |
| 31st | 05.49 | 21.06 | 05.11 | 20.46 |

J

## THE SEA

### Average sea temperature

| | |
|---|---|
| Orkney: | 12.9°C |
| South Shields: | 15.1°C |
| Carrickfergus: | 13.6°C |
| Lowestoft: | 15.2°C |
| Aberystwyth: | 12.7°C |
| Bantry: | 15.2°C |
| Cowes: | 15.2°C |
| Penzance: | 16.4°C |

### Spring and neap tides

The spring tides are the most extreme tides of the month, with the highest rises and falls, and the neap tides are the least extreme, with the smallest. Exact timings vary around the coast, but expect them around the following dates:

**Spring tides:** 11th–12th and 26th–27th

**Neap tides:** 3rd–4th and 19th–20th

In the tide timetable opposite, spring tides are shown with an asterisk.

## July tide timetable for Dover

For guidance on how to convert this for your local area, see page 8.

|  | High water | | Low water | |
|---|---|---|---|---|
|  | Morning | Afternoon | Morning | Afternoon |
| 1st | 04.42 | 16.59 | 11.58 | — |
| 2nd | 05.36 | 17.53 | 00.28 | 12.45 |
| 3rd | 06.37 | 18.53 | 01.19 | 13.40 |
| 4th | 07.43 | 20.00 | 02.15 | 14.40 |
| 5th | 08.46 | 21.03 | 03.12 | 15.39 |
| 6th | 09.40 | 21.57 | 04.08 | 16.35 |
| 7th | 10.27 | 22.43 | 04.59 | 17.25 |
| 8th | 11.08 | 23.22 | 05.46 | 18.08 |
| 9th | 11.46 | 23.58 | 06.29 | 18.49 |
| 10th | — | 12.21 | 07.09 | 19.29 |
| 11th | 00.33 | 12.55 | 07.49 | 20.09 * |
| 12th | 01.08 | 13.29 | 08.28 | 20.49 * |
| 13th | 01.43 | 14.04 | 09.07 | 21.29 |
| 14th | 02.19 | 14.42 | 09.44 | 22.09 |
| 15th | 02.58 | 15.25 | 10.22 | 22.49 |
| 16th | 03.43 | 16.13 | 11.02 | 23.34 |
| 17th | 04.36 | 17.08 | 11.49 | — |
| 18th | 05.38 | 18.12 | 00.26 | 12.47 |
| 19th | 06.54 | 19.25 | 01.29 | 13.58 |
| 20th | 08.13 | 20.40 | 02.39 | 15.11 |
| 21st | 09.22 | 21.48 | 03.49 | 16.22 |
| 22nd | 10.24 | 22.51 | 05.00 | 17.33 |
| 23rd | 11.19 | 23.48 | 06.13 | 18.40 |
| 24th | — | 12.09 | 07.17 | 19.39 |
| 25th | 00.37 | 12.53 | 08.11 | 20.31 |
| 26th | 01.21 | 13.36 | 08.57 | 21.17 * |
| 27th | 02.03 | 14.17 | 09.38 | 21.58 * |
| 28th | 02.44 | 14.58 | 10.13 | 22.35 |
| 29th | 03.24 | 15.39 | 10.45 | 23.08 |
| 30th | 04.06 | 16.21 | 11.13 | 23.40 |
| 31st | 04.51 | 17.06 | 11.43 | — |

J

# A SEA SHANTY FOR JULY

### Santiana

A song for St Anne's feast day, on 26th July. There is confusion about the origins and meaning of this shanty, which may have had an African American tune at its birth. It could be about the 19th-century Mexican general Santa Anna, in whose army many British sailors deserted their ships to fight, or it might be for St Anne, the patron saint of sailors and the protector from storms. Either way, it apparently made its way inland from US coastal ports and became as popular among cowboys as it was among sailors.

This is a pump shanty, used when pumping water out of the hulls of leaky wooden ships, a frequent and exhausting job much improved by the singing of a shanty.

I'd give her whisky an' lots o' gin
*Hooray Santiana!*
And stay in the port where she was in
*Heave away to the plains of Mexico!*

Though times are hard an' wages low
*Hooray Santiana!*
'Tis time for us to roll an' go
*Heave away to the plains of Mexico!*

Oh, Mexico, where the land lies low
*Hooray Santiana!*
Oh, Mexico, where the wind don't blow
*Heave away to the plains of Mexico!*

J

A MAP OF
MACKEREL
· MIGRATION ·

# MIGRATION OF THE MONTH

### Mackerel

Our coasts are circled by several swirling, silvery masses of mackerel, and all of them are currently on the move. North East Atlantic mackerel comprise three distinct populations, genetically identical but all with different spawning and overwintering grounds. The first, the North Sea component, overwinters in deep water to the east and north of Shetland and on the edge of the Norwegian Deep, an area of sea off the Norwegian coast where the seabed drops to a vast and cavernous 700m depth. In the spring this mass of fish migrated to the central part of the North Sea east of England to spawn. Meanwhile the Western component spent winter near the Continental Shelf to the west, migrating to south and west of the British Isles to spawn in spring. And finally the Southern component overwintered in the Bay of Biscay west of France and started to spawn there in the relatively warm water as early as January, migrating up to the Irish Sea and along the southern coast of England through spring. Having no swim bladder, they cannot stop swimming – the swift of the sea – and one tagged fish was found to have travelled over 1,200km in 13 days.

Female mackerel start to spawn at two years old and produce up to twenty batches of spawn through their spawning period, spawning as they travel. Although mackerel make full use of the water column, from the surface to the depths, they spawn in the warmer waters near the surface, and this is where the eggs and later the larvae will float, drifting passively until they develop into juveniles. Then they will begin to undertake vertical migrations from the surface to deeper water, feasting on zooplankton, before later joining the mass migration.

# THE GARDEN

### July garden meditation

Although we are past the summer solstice, we are not past the summer. The land's thermal lag means that the earth beneath our feet has taken time to warm up since the beginning of the year, but it has been storing up the sun's heat all along and now the warmest two months of the year are here. Step out into the garden, remove your shoes, and let the soles of your feet connect with that stored warmth. Try going barefoot on the pavement a little, too, for fun.

In July, trees start to take on their high summer colour, a lovely, rich mid-green, and the sight of a mature tree in July waving its branches in a summer breeze against a deep blue sky is one of the best sights in the world. Note and enjoy this now, even if you can only see the tips of your tree across the rooftops. And that breeze. Close your eyes and notice how warm it is, how little you are clenched and braced against it, how relaxed your body can be as it moves around you.

Think about the subtle switch that the garden has just made, from the lush green young growth and flowers of spring and midsummer, to the start of ripening. Suddenly the garden is providing bucketloads of produce, and the brambles stop flowering and start making tight little green berries. Look for evidence of this change in your garden, as the year turns.

## Jobs in the garden

- Pinch out the sideshoots on your tomato plants, otherwise they will take off and become as big as the plant itself. You should be feeding your tomatoes every week now.
- Give your pond a little attention. Top it up if it needs it, ideally with rainwater from a water butt, and remove blanketweed.
- Cut back the gangly foliage of your hardy geraniums now. They will then put on a neat little mound of leaves, hopefully followed quickly by a second flush of flowers.

## How much to sow

It is tempting to sow whole packets of seeds and then be overwhelmed by seedlings or, later, great gluts of one type of vegetable. This guide will help you to sow roughly the amount you need for a family of four; adjust to suit your own circumstances and favourites. In every case, sow a small number more than suggested to allow for non-germination and seedling failure.

**Carrots:** Make a direct sowing, 3m long, of a maincrop variety for winter.

**Beetroot and turnips:** Make a direct sowing of a 3-m row of each for winter.

**Spinach and Swiss chard:** Direct sow 3m of each.

**Herbs:** For autumn and winter, sow 1m each of chervil, coriander, parsley and rocket.

# THE KITCHEN

### Romani recipe for July – Pickled nasturtiums

Nasturtiums are starting to set their chunky round seeds now. Gathered and pickled they are a little like capers. Recipe based on the research of Romani and Traveller historian Robert Dawson.

Gather the green seeds of nasturtiums. Pack them in a sterilised jar and pour on boiling apple cider vinegar. After a few weeks they will make a nice pickle for meat dishes.

### In season

### In the hedgerows, woods and fields
**Wild herbs:** As for June (see page 132)
**Edible wild flowers:** As for June (see page 132), plus chamomile and nasturtium (flowers and seeds)
**Wild fruits and nuts:** Wild strawberries, cherry plum, wild gooseberry, green walnuts for pickling
**Game:** Wood pigeon

### From the seashore and rivers
Samphire
**Fish and shellfish:** Mackerel, brown crab, herring, lobster, turbot, sea trout, black bream, sea bass, sardine, salmon

### From the kitchen garden
**Vegetables:** As for June (see page 133), except asparagus is now over, plus French beans, runner beans, fennel and shallots
**Fruits:** Gooseberries, loganberries, raspberries, cherries, blueberries, blackcurrants
**Herbs:** Mint, basil, dill, chives, marjoram, thyme, oregano
**Edible flowers:** Calendula flowers, nasturtium flowers and seeds

### From the farms
Cherries, fresh goat's milk cheeses, ewe's curd, ricotta, lamb

### And traditional imports
Apricots, peaches, nectarines and cherries

# RECIPES

### Grilled herby mackerel with Russian salad

This salad is full of summer vegetables jumbled together and is the perfect summery accompaniment to grilled fresh mackerel.

Serves 4

Ingredients

*For the salad*

200g waxy potatoes, boiled, cooled and cut into small cubes

100g carrots, boiled, cooled and cut into small cubes

100g peas, cooked and cooled

100g green beans, cooked, cooled and cut into short lengths

1 gherkin, or 8 cornichons, finely chopped

2 tablespoons capers

4 anchovy fillets, finely chopped

Handful of finely chopped parsley

Small handful of finely snipped chives

4 tablespoons mayonnaise

Salt and pepper

*For the mackerel*

4 whole mackerel, gutted, descaled and cleaned

Bunch of dill

Bunch of mint

1 lemon, sliced

Olive oil for drizzling

Sea salt

## Method

Tip all of the salad ingredients into a large bowl and mix well, then season with salt and pepper. Refrigerate until you are ready to serve.

Wash the fish well, pat dry and make slashes in the skin on each side, then fill the cavity with the herbs and lemon slices, and place on a grill pan. Drizzle with olive oil and sprinkle with sea salt, then grill for a few minutes on one side. Turn the mackerel over, drizzle with more olive oil, and sprinkle sea salt over it before grilling for another few minutes until cooked.

Serve the fish alongside a good spoonful of the salad.

### Raspberry, ginger and hibiscus switchel (haymakers' punch)

Switchel, or haymakers' punch, is claimed by both the Caribbean and New England and dates from the 17th century.

| Yield 1.1 litres |
| --- |
| **Ingredients** |
| 4 slices fresh ginger |
| 50g raspberries, crushed |
| Juice of 1 lemon |
| 2 tablespoons apple cider vinegar |
| 1 tablespoon honey |
| A pinch of dried hibiscus petal |

## Method

Pour 250ml water into a pot and heat to boiling point with the fresh ginger; simmer for a few minutes. Leave to cool completely and pour into a large sterilised jar. Add a further 750ml water and the remaining ingredients, and stir well. Refrigerate for 24 hours and then serve. It will keep for about a week.

# PILGRIMAGE OF THE MONTH

## The Hajj

One of the great pilgrimages of the world, the Hajj is a pilgrimage to Mecca attended annually by more than two million Muslims, including twenty-five thousand from the United Kingdom. It takes place from the 8th to the 13th of the Islamic month of Dhu al-Hijjah, which means that this year it occurs from the 19th to the 23rd of July.

The origins of the Hajj lie with Ibrahim. (Also known as Abraham, he was the father of monotheism – the belief in the existence of one god.) Ibrahim took his wife, Hajar, and baby son, Ishmail, to a deserted valley in what is now Saudi Arabia and left them there, trusting in God to take care of them. Ishmail cried with thirst, and Hajar ran between the hills looking for water. She prayed to God, and in response to her prayers the angel Jibril touched the earth and a spring of fresh water appeared, the Well of Zamzam. Over time the city of Mecca grew up, and close to the well Ibrahim and Ishmail built the Kaabah, the House of God, a cube-shaped building that all Muslims orient themselves towards when praying.

In 632 the Prophet Muhammad visited Mecca and found that idols of many gods had been erected around the site of the Kaabah. He destroyed the idols, rededicated the site to Allah and led the first pilgrimage. The same path is followed by pilgrims today. They dress in simple white clothing called Ihram and first visit the Masjid al-Haram (Great Mosque of Mecca), which surrounds the Kaabah, to perform the initial Tawaf, circling the Kaabah anticlockwise seven times. Then they perform the Sa'ee, hurrying between the small hills of Safa and Marwah seven times, just as Hajar did when looking for water. Next they travel to the plain of Mina to a vast tent city to camp, and from there to the plain of Arafat where they spend the day in supplication and prayer. Back at Mina they must throw seven pebbles at three stone pillars representing the devil, who tried to dissuade Ibrahim from offering his son for sacrifice. Then there is the sacrifice of a goat, the meat shared. Finally the pilgrims return to Mecca for the final Sa'ee and Tawaf.

# August

 Lammas (Christian) and Lughnasadh (Gaelic/pagan/neopagan)

 August bank holiday, Scotland, Republic of Ireland

 6th–30th: Edinburgh Festival Fringe

 Olympics closing ceremony, Japan

 Al Hijra – Islamic New Year, start of the year 1443 (Muslim) – festivities begin at sundown the night before

 The Glorious Twelfth – grouse-shooting season begins

 The Assumption of Mary (Christian)

 28th–30th: Notting Hill Carnival, London

 August bank holiday, England, Wales, Northern Ireland

 Krishna Janmashtami – Krishna's Birthday (Hindu)

# ROMANI NAME FOR THE MONTH

## Giveskero – month of the corn

In the Romani year August was the month of the corn, which means that it is time for the wheat to be brought in (corn having always been used as a generic term for cereal, rather than meaning sweetcorn). The wheat harvest has long been the biggest event in the rural year. Whole rural families would move from farm to farm around their village to help harvest the wheat, and there are a great number of traditions associated with it. This is particularly the case at the end of the harvest, when a corn dolly would be made from the last sheaf cut and would keep the 'spirit of the corn' or the 'corn mother' safe throughout the winter; the following spring, the corn dolly would be buried in the field as it was ploughed and sown.

And, of course, Romani families were a part of this, coming from further afield than the locals, but travelling in their regular route around the seasonal harvests to set up camp in a tucked-away corner of a ripe cornfield. The fields were ready for harvesting when the wheat turned from green to golden, and the heads began to nod. The wheat was cut with scythes and then gathered into sheafs and bundled onto carts to be taken away, threshed and ground. Wheat harvests were renowned for hard work and hard play, and after the day's work was done the families would light a fire, cook food and then possibly pull out a board for some traditional step-dancing, taking it in turns to sing and dance by the firelight into the late summer night.

# THE MOON

## Moon phases

New moon – 8th August, 14.50

1st quarter – 15th August, 16.20

Full moon – 22nd August, 13.02

3rd quarter – 30th August, 08.13

## Gardening by the moon

**3rd quarter to new moon: 1st–8th and 30th–31st.** Prune. Harvest for storage. Fertilise and mulch the soil.

**New moon to 1st quarter: 8th–15th.** Sow crops that develop below ground. Dig the soil.

**1st quarter to full moon: 15th–22nd.** Sow crops that develop above ground. Plant seedlings and young plants.

**Full moon to 3rd quarter: 22nd–30th.** Harvest crops for immediate eating. Harvest fruit.

A

## Moon sign – Leo

Astrologers believe that the new moon is a time to make plans and focus on your dreams and hopes for the period ahead, and that each new moon has a particular energy, depending on which zodiacal sign it is in. The new moon on the 8th will be in Leo, which is an energetic and confident sign, making this a good time for projects that involve self-promotion, celebration and fun.

### Navigating by the stars, sun and moon

### Use the sun to hold a bearing

This will not help you to find your direction using the sun (for that, see Find East and West Using the Moon, page 98) but rather will help you to keep it. It is used by mountain rescue teams so that they can keep their bearing while searching, without having to refer to a compass repeatedly. It will stop you going round in circles. Face the direction in which you want to travel and put your arm out straight above you, holding it so you block the sun from your eyes. Hold your arm in that position for ten seconds, so that you imprint a good sense of where the sun should be in relation to you. Lower your arm and move forward, always keeping the sun in that spot. If the sun is behind you, take the bearing from your shadow. Put your arm out parallel with your shadow for a minute, and then as you move keep your shadow in that position. You can travel on this bearing for ten minutes before you need to stop and take the bearing again. You can do the same with a bright moon but you'll need to retake your bearing more often, as the moon moves faster across the sky.

## Moon rise and set

| | St Michael's Mount | | Hopton-on-Sea | | |
|---|---|---|---|---|---|
| | Rise | Set | Rise | Set | |
| 1st | 00.21 | 15.18 | — | 14.56 | |
| 2nd | 00.41 | 16.26 | 00.03 | 16.06 | |
| 3rd | 01.06 | 17.32 | 00.25 | 17.15 | |
| 4th | 01.37 | 18.35 | 00.54 | 18.20 | |
| 5th | 02.17 | 19.31 | 01.32 | 19.16 | |
| 6th | 03.08 | 20.18 | 02.23 | 20.03 | |
| 7th | 04.10 | 20.56 | 03.26 | 20.38 | |
| 8th | 05.20 | 21.25 | 04.38 | 21.06 | new moon |
| 9th | 06.35 | 21.49 | 05.56 | 21.27 | |
| 10th | 07.52 | 22.09 | 07.16 | 21.45 | |
| 11th | 09.10 | 22.27 | 08.37 | 22.00 | |
| 12th | 10.28 | 22.45 | 09.58 | 22.15 | |
| 13th | 11.48 | 23.03 | 11.20 | 22.30 | |
| 14th | 13.08 | 23.23 | 12.43 | 22.47 | |
| 15th | 14.31 | 23.48 | 14.09 | 23.09 | 1st quarter |
| 16th | 15.54 | — | 15.35 | 23.38 | |
| 17th | 17.14 | 00.20 | 16.58 | — | |
| 18th | 18.24 | 01.02 | 18.10 | 00.18 | |
| 19th | 19.22 | 01.59 | 19.07 | 01.13 | |
| 20th | 20.05 | 03.08 | 19.48 | 02.23 | |
| 21st | 20.37 | 04.26 | 20.18 | 03.43 | |
| 22nd | 21.01 | 05.46 | 20.39 | 05.06 | full moon |
| 23rd | 21.21 | 07.05 | 20.56 | 06.28 | |
| 24th | 21.38 | 08.21 | 21.10 | 07.47 | |
| 25th | 21.53 | 09.34 | 21.23 | 09.03 | |
| 26th | 22.09 | 10.44 | 21.36 | 10.16 | |
| 27th | 22.25 | 11.54 | 21.50 | 11.28 | |
| 28th | 22.43 | 13.03 | 22.06 | 12.40 | |
| 29th | 23.06 | 14.12 | 22.26 | 13.51 | |
| 30th | 23.34 | 15.19 | 22.52 | 15.01 | 3rd quarter |
| 31st | — | 16.24 | 23.26 | 16.08 | |

Where moonset times are before moonrise times, this is the setting of the previous night's moon.

# THE SKY

## At night

**2nd–3rd:** Saturn is at opposition, at its closest and brightest for this year. Rises at 21.00 in the southeast, reaching a maximum altitude of 20 degrees at 01.00 in the south and setting at 05.00 in the southwest.

**11th:** Close approach of Venus and the moon, visible in the dusk from about 20.30 in the west at an altitude of 11 degrees, until setting at 21.30 in the west.

**12th–13th:** Perseids meteor shower. The radiant will be at about 40 degrees in the northeast at midnight.

**20th:** Jupiter is at opposition. Rises at 20.30 in the southeast, reaching a maximum altitude of 24 degrees at 01.00 in the south and setting at 05.30 in the southwest.

**20th–21st:** Close approach of Saturn and the moon, with Jupiter nearby, rising at 20.30 in the southeast, reaching a maximum altitude of 16 degrees in the south at 23.30 and setting at 03.30 in the southwest.

**21st–22nd:** Close approach of Jupiter and the moon, rising at 21.00 in the southeast, reaching an altitude of 24 degrees in the south at 01.00 and setting at 05.00 in the southwest.

## By day

**21st:** At solar midday (approximately 13.00 BST/IST) the sun reaches an altitude of 51 degrees at Lee-on-the-Solent in Hampshire and 44 degrees at Lairg in Scotland.

**1st:** Earliest sunrise, St Michael's Mount (05.50) and Hopton-on-Sea (05.12).

**1st:** Latest sunset, St Michael's Mount (21.04) and Hopton-on-Sea (20.44).

**1st–31st:** Daylight decreases by 1h 41m at St Michael's Mount and by 1h 51m at Hopton-on-Sea.

## Sunrise and set

| | *St Michael's Mount* | | *Hopton-on-Sea* | |
| | Rise | Set | Rise | Set |
| --- | --- | --- | --- | --- |
| 1st | 05.50 | 21.04 | 05.12 | 20.44 |
| 2nd | 05.52 | 21.02 | 05.14 | 20.43 |
| 3rd | 05.53 | 21.01 | 05.16 | 20.41 |
| 4th | 05.55 | 20.59 | 05.17 | 20.39 |
| 5th | 05.56 | 20.58 | 05.19 | 20.37 |
| 6th | 05.58 | 20.56 | 05.20 | 20.35 |
| 7th | 05.59 | 20.54 | 05.22 | 20.33 |
| 8th | 06.01 | 20.52 | 05.24 | 20.32 |
| 9th | 06.02 | 20.51 | 05.25 | 20.30 |
| 10th | 06.04 | 20.49 | 05.27 | 20.28 |
| 11th | 06.05 | 20.47 | 05.29 | 20.26 |
| 12th | 06.07 | 20.45 | 05.30 | 20.24 |
| 13th | 06.08 | 20.43 | 05.32 | 20.22 |
| 14th | 06.09 | 20.42 | 05.34 | 20.20 |
| 15th | 06.11 | 20.40 | 05.35 | 20.18 |
| 16th | 06.12 | 20.38 | 05.37 | 20.16 |
| 17th | 06.14 | 20.36 | 05.39 | 20.13 |
| 18th | 06.15 | 20.34 | 05.40 | 20.11 |
| 19th | 06.17 | 20.32 | 05.42 | 20.09 |
| 20th | 06.18 | 20.30 | 05.44 | 20.07 |
| 21st | 06.20 | 20.28 | 05.45 | 20.05 |
| 22nd | 06.21 | 20.26 | 05.47 | 20.03 |
| 23rd | 06.23 | 20.24 | 05.49 | 20.01 |
| 24th | 06.24 | 20.22 | 05.50 | 19.58 |
| 25th | 06.26 | 20.20 | 05.52 | 19.56 |
| 26th | 06.27 | 20.18 | 05.54 | 19.54 |
| 27th | 06.29 | 20.16 | 05.55 | 19.52 |
| 28th | 06.30 | 20.14 | 05.57 | 19.49 |
| 29th | 06.32 | 20.12 | 05.59 | 19.47 |
| 30th | 06.33 | 20.09 | 06.00 | 19.45 |
| 31st | 06.35 | 20.07 | 06.02 | 19.43 |

A

# THE SEA

## Average sea temperature

| | |
|---|---|
| Orkney: | 13.2°C |
| South Shields: | 15.6°C |
| Carrickfergus: | 14.2°C |
| Lowestoft: | 16.6°C |
| Aberystwyth: | 15.5°C |
| Bantry: | 16.1°C |
| Cowes: | 16.7°C |
| Penzance: | 16.9°C |

## Spring and neap tides

The spring tides are the most extreme tides of the month, with the highest rises and falls, and the neap tides are the least extreme, with the smallest. Exact timings vary around the coast, but expect them around the following dates:

**Spring tides:** 11th–12th and 24th–25th

**Neap tides:** 2nd–3rd and 17th–18th

In the tide timetable opposite, spring tides are shown with an asterisk.

## August tide timetable for Dover

For guidance on how to convert this for your local area, see page 8.

| | High water | | Low water | |
| --- | --- | --- | --- | --- |
| | Morning | Afternoon | Morning | Afternoon |
| 1st | 05.43 | 17.58 | 00.15 | 12.23 |
| 2nd | 06.45 | 19.02 | 01.05 | 13.25 |
| 3rd | 07.53 | 20.12 | 02.13 | 14.44 |
| 4th | 08.59 | 21.18 | 03.22 | 15.54 |
| 5th | 09.56 | 22.12 | 04.23 | 16.52 |
| 6th | 10.42 | 22.56 | 05.17 | 17.42 |
| 7th | 11.21 | 23.35 | 06.05 | 18.28 |
| 8th | 11.57 | — | 06.50 | 19.12 |
| 9th | 00.12 | 12.33 | 07.33 | 19.55 |
| 10th | 00.48 | 13.08 | 08.15 | 20.37 |
| 11th | 01.24 | 13.45 | 08.54 | 21.16 * |
| 12th | 02.00 | 14.22 | 09.30 | 21.54 * |
| 13th | 02.37 | 15.02 | 10.05 | 22.30 |
| 14th | 03.19 | 15.47 | 10.42 | 23.10 |
| 15th | 04.07 | 16.38 | 11.24 | 23.56 |
| 16th | 05.05 | 17.41 | — | 12.16 |
| 17th | 06.23 | 19.02 | 00.56 | 13.26 * |
| 18th | 07.59 | 20.34 | 02.12 | 14.49 * |
| 19th | 09.18 | 21.53 | 03.34 | 16.12 |
| 20th | 10.23 | 22.58 | 04.59 | 17.34 |
| 21st | 11.17 | 23.50 | 06.16 | 18.41 |
| 22nd | — | 12.01 | 07.13 | 19.34 |
| 23rd | 00.32 | 12.40 | 08.01 | 20.21 |
| 24th | 01.09 | 13.19 | 08.40 | 21.00 |
| 25th | 01.44 | 13.56 | 09.14 | 21.33 |
| 26th | 02.18 | 14.32 | 09.42 | 22.01 |
| 27th | 02.52 | 15.06 | 10.04 | 22.24 |
| 28th | 03.25 | 15.38 | 10.24 | 22.45 |
| 29th | 04.00 | 16.11 | 10.49 | 23.13 |
| 30th | 04.42 | 16.55 | 11.24 | 23.53 |
| 31st | 05.50 | 18.11 | — | 12.12 |

# A SEA SHANTY FOR AUGUST

### The Oak and the Ash

Shanties are far less seasonal than landlubber folk songs, perhaps because the weather in the Atlantic was either cold and wet or really cold and wet. However, in this West Country shanty we do hear that the oak, ash and elm trees are all in leaf and so we can safely assume that it is summer, at least in this homesick sailor's imagination. This is a fo'c's'cle, or forebitter, shanty, sung in the sailors' downtime, as such yearning songs often seem to have been.

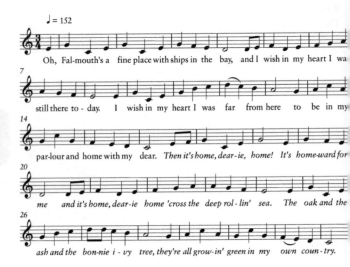

In Plymouth out walking a girl I did meet.
She carried a babe as she walked through the street,
And I thought of the young maid who once caught my eye,
When I left her some silver, a cradle to buy.
*Then it's home, dearie, home! It's homeward for me*
*And it's home, dearie, home 'cross the deep rollin' sea.*
*The oak and the ash and the bonnie ivy tree,*
*They're all growin' green in my own country.*

And if it's a girl she will stay here with me,
And if it's a boy he will plough the blue sea.
He'll plough the blue sea as his daddy had done
With his pea jacket blue like a true sailor's son.
*Then it's home...*

A

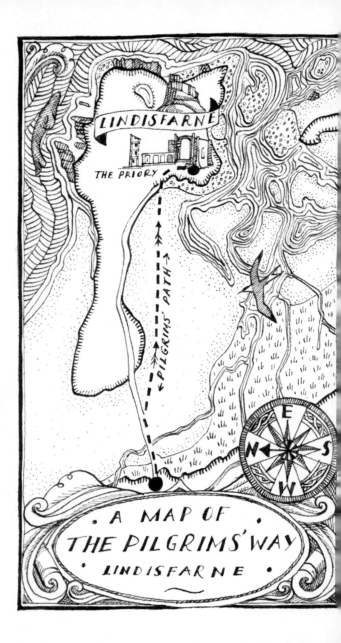

LINDISFARNE

THE PRIORY

← PILGRIMS' PATH →

A MAP OF
THE PILGRIMS' WAY
LINDISFARNE

# PILGRIMAGE OF THE MONTH

## Pilgrims' Way, Lindisfarne, for the Feast of St Aidan

Stretching out across Beal Sands on the Northumberland coast
is a line of poles 3.5m high, set into the sand. They follow a
route trodden by saints and pilgrims for at least 1,500 years,
5km across the mudflats towards Lindisfarne, or Holy Island.
This is a tidal pilgrimage, washed over by the sea and visited
by seals twice a day, and you must time your visit carefully if
you wish to walk, setting out on the falling tide. Summer is a
good bet, as it is warm enough to walk barefoot, which is the
recommended way: in places the mud can be up to 30cm deep
so if you insist on footwear you will either ruin your walking
boots or lose your wellies.

31st August is the feast day of St Aidan, the Apostle
of Northumbria. Aidan, who was of Irish descent, was a
monk brought from the Isle of Iona by Oswald, King of
Northumbria, who tasked Aidan with restoring Christianity to
the Anglo-Saxons. The religion had been brought to Britain by
the Romans, but by 634, on this northeast coast of England, it
had been largely displaced by Anglo-Saxon paganism. Aidan
founded a priory on Lindisfarne and travelled extensively
through Northumbria, spreading the gospel among aristocracy
and the poor alike. The site of the original priory is now a
church, rebuilt by the Normans, and the oldest structure on the
island – its remains can be visited.

The origin of the name Lindisfarne is uncertain but 'lindis'
may refer to the people of the Kingdom of Lindsey, which
is part of modern Lincolnshire, and 'farne' may come from
Old English *fearena*, which means 'traveller', underlining
Lindisfarne's position as an ancient place of pilgrimage.
There are various long-distance pilgrimage routes that lead
here, including St Oswald's Way, stretching from Hadrian's
Wall, and St Cuthbert's Way, named after the second Bishop
of Lindisfarne and stretching from Melrose in the Scottish
borders. All end up on this otherworldly stretch of sand and
mud, the wind whipping in from the North Sea and the cries
of gulls in the air.

A

# THE GARDEN

## August garden meditation

There is a slide towards mellowness in the garden now, the weather is warm and easy, but there are hints of gold creeping into the edges of the garden. The long grasses are turning straw-like and the berries have started to swell. Stand or sit outside for a few minutes and look for signs that your garden has moved into the harvest phase of the year: even if you do not have a vegetable patch you will be able to see it. But if you do, pick a tomato, while it's still warm from the sun, and as you pop it into your mouth think about how all of its sugars have been laid down by a summer's worth of sunlight. This is another of the easy months in which to be barefoot, so go for it, feeling the connection to the earth that it brings. The ground should be at its warmest now, still releasing the sunshine it has been soaking up since spring. If it has been wet, think about the worms and other organisms in the soil and how loosely and easily they can move through it. If dry, think about the deep wells of moisture held down below in the subsoil, which at this very moment the trees and shrubs are stretching their delicate roots out to reach. Trees have taken on their deep green late-summer foliage, matt and rough. Think about what has turned the leaves this way since they emerged: sunshine, wind, nibbling insects. They have seen some things.

## Jobs in the garden

- Feed your dahlias with an organic tomato fertiliser to encourage more flowers, and make sure they are well propped up. Pick off the spent flowers.
- Trim hedges and topiary in late August and they should look good for winter.
- Water camellias and rhododendrons well, particularly those in pots. This is when they form their flower buds so a dry spell now can mean no flowers next spring.

## How much to sow

It is tempting to sow whole packets of seeds and then be overwhelmed by seedlings or, later, great gluts of one type of vegetable. This guide will help you to sow roughly the amount you need for a family of four; adjust to suit your own circumstances and favourites. In every case, sow a small number more than suggested to allow for non-germination and seedling failure.

**Winter salads:** Start sowing winter salads such as corn salad, winter purslane and land cress direct into the soil, a 2-m row of each.

**Oriental leaves:** Sow direct: mizuna, mibuna, pak choi, red mustard, a 2-m row of each.

**Spring onion, rocket, radish and hardy winter lettuce:** Sow 1m of each.

**Herbs:** For autumn and winter, sow 1m each of chervil, coriander, parsley and rocket.

**Root crops:** Last chance to sow root crops for winter: beetroot, turnip and autumn varieties of carrots, a 3-m row of each.

**Spring greens:** Sow 30 plants direct or under cover.

A

# THE KITCHEN

### Romani recipe for August – Bread and butter pudding

Mark the month of the corn, Lammas and the new season's wheat with a bread and butter pudding, cooked over the fire. You might push a few blackberries between each slice too, if you have them. Recipe based on the research of Romani and Traveller historian Robert Dawson.

You will need 6–9 slices of bread (depending on the size of your loaf and the size of your baking tin), 200g sultanas and currants, 225g sugar, 5 large eggs and 400ml milk. Remove the crusts from the bread slices and butter the slices on both sides. Grease an ovenproof dish and line the bottom with bread, then sprinkle over half the dried fruit and a spoonful of the sugar. Add another layer of bread, and spread the rest of the fruit over it with another spoonful of sugar. Top with a final layer of bread. Beat the eggs, milk and remaining sugar together, then pour over the top, leaving it to soak in for 30 minutes. Cover with foil and cook in a Dutch oven over a medium heat for 45 minutes – or in a moderate oven – and then cook uncovered for a further 15 minutes.

### In season

### In the hedgerows, woods and fields
**Wild herbs:** Cleavers, hairy bittercress, hedge garlic, lemon balm, marjoram, spearmint, sweet cicely, watercress, water mint, wild thyme, wild fennel
**Edible wild flowers:** Broom, borage, chamomile, honeysuckle, marigold, meadowsweet, nasturtium (and their seeds), red clover, wild rose
**Wild fruits and nuts:** Cherry plum, wild strawberries, bilberries, blackberries, rosehips, rowan berries, wild gooseberry, cobnuts
**Game:** Grouse, ptarmigan, snipe, wood pigeon

**From the seashore and rivers**
**Fish and shellfish:** Black bream, brown crab, herring, lobster, mackerel, sea trout, turbot, plaice, sardines, megrim sole, squid, salmon
Samphire, sea buckthorn

**From the kitchen garden**
**Vegetables:** Sweetcorn, tomatoes, aubergines, French beans, runner beans, calabrese, fennel, courgettes, leeks, radishes, globe artichokes, beetroot, cabbages, carrots, cauliflower, chard, cucumber, endive, garlic, lettuce, shallots, onions, spring onions, sweet peppers, chilli peppers, peas, potatoes, wild rocket, spinach, turnips
**Fruits:** Plums, apples, pears, blackcurrants, blueberries, loganberries, melons, raspberries, redcurrants, strawberries, cherries
**Herbs:** Marjoram, thyme, dill, basil, mint, oregano

**From the farms**
Cobnuts, cherries

A

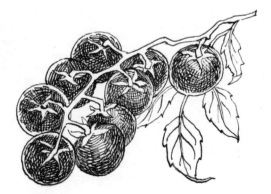

## RECIPES

### Samphire and burrata

During its brief summer season, samphire is almost always eaten with fish, as its salty, succulent stems complement seafood perfectly. But this is my favourite way to eat it: hot, salty, garlicky samphire against cool, creamy burrata, the juices mopped up with a hunk of bread. I owe credit for this to my friend Ellen Hughes, who threw it together one sunny lunchtime and got me instantly hooked.

| Serves 2 |
| --- |
| **Ingredients** |
| 50g butter |
| 150g samphire, washed and trimmed |
| 1 clove garlic, crushed |
| Juice of half a lemon |
| 1 burrata |
| Pepper |
| Soft white bread, to serve |

**Method**

Melt the butter in a frying pan over a moderate heat, and tip in the samphire and the garlic, stirring all together until the garlic is cooked and the samphire is softened and takes on a slightly glassy look. Squeeze over the lemon juice and add a few grinds of pepper, then stir and remove from the heat. Lift the samphire out with 2 forks and divide it between 2 bowls. Split the burrata between the bowls and then pour the hot, lemony, garlicky butter over it. Eat immediately, using the bread to get every bit of sauce.

# MIGRATION OF THE MONTH

## Dragonfly migration

This month the ponds and lakes of southern England will be visited by quivering and vibrant blue and black dragonflies, hovering and shooting suddenly away, or barrelling headlong through the air, their glassy wings glinting in the sun. These are migrant hawker dragonflies, and they are summer visitors.

Insect migrations are very little understood, partly because it is so hard to track the movements of such tiny creatures. We only really know that dragonflies migrate because several non-native species suddenly appear in summer, including the red-veined darter, the lesser emperor, the vagrant emperor and the migrant hawker, which have been visiting for many years but are now seen in greater numbers. New dragonfly species have colonised Britain in the last 20 years, including the willow emerald damselfly and the small red-eyed damselfly. The dainty damselfly has returned, having last been seen here in 1953. There was a single confirmed sighting of the migrant hawker in the 20th century; just four were spotted in southern England in 2006, and then a good number in 2010, particularly in south Essex and north Kent. Numbers are now increasing every year.

Unfortunately, this increase in numbers is down to climate change. Dragonflies cannot regulate their body temperature and so, as the climate heats up, they need to move to cooler areas in order to survive. There are major shifts in dragonfly ranges across the whole world. It seems likely that as temperatures rise and mainland Europe becomes too hot for many of them in summer, we will see more migrant dragonflies flitting across the English Channel.

Dragonflies can live up to four years, but most of this time is spent as nymphs, living in water. When they are fully grown and the weather is right, they will climb up a stem and complete their metamorphosis, shedding their skin, pumping up their wings and setting off to look for food and a mate. Once mated, the female will find a calm body of water in which to lay her eggs, and the cycle begins again.

A

# September

 Start of meteorological autumn

 Rosh Hashanah – Jewish New Year, start of Jewish year 5782 – festivities begin the night before

 Ganesh Chaturthi – the birth of Ganesh (Hindu)

 Enkutatash – Ethiopean New Year (Rastafarian)

 Yom Kippur – Day of Atonement (Jewish)

 Sukkot – First day of Tabernacles (Jewish)

 Autumnal equinox – start of astronomical autumn

 Mabon – harvest celebration (neopagan)

 Michaelmas Day (Christian, traditional)

# ROMANI NAME FOR THE MONTH

## Rigerimaskero – month of the gathering

This is such an abundant month that in the Romani language the name for the month is a reflection of this abundance, as it translates as month of the gathering, or of the harvests. This would have meant two things to the Romani. On the one hand it entailed further travelling to help farmers bring in their harvests before the weather turned cool. In *Our Forgotten Years*, Romani writer and activist Maggie Smith-Bendell writes of her family travelling to Ledbury every autumn to take part in the hop harvest, which lasted a full five weeks through September and part of October. She recalls pulling into a field full of other Traveller families, seeing fires flaring up with black pots set over them, and remembers that the farmer would put out stacks of logs for the Romani families to use, and would provide them with eggs, butter and milk at a small charge. There were also wild rabbits to be caught to stew with vegetables over the fire as the weather turned colder.

And then there was also the hedgerow harvest to gather in. Living so fully in the landscape, the Romanies have always made use of wild harvests, and this month, golden with late-summer sunshine and with just a hint of autumnal cool in the air, there would have been blackberries and elderberries glistening and hazelnuts turning toasty brown in the hedgerows by the side of the road. All in all, this was an abundant time of year, with plenty of food to gather up and bring home to the family wagon, as well as providing plenty of agricultural work to help fill the family coffers.

# THE MOON

## Moon phases

New moon – 7th September, 01.52

1st quarter – 13th September, 21.39

Full moon – 21st September, 00.55*

3rd quarter – 29th September, 02.57

## Gardening by the moon

**3rd quarter to new moon: 1st–7th and 29th–30th.** Prune. Harvest for storage. Fertilise and mulch the soil.

**New moon to 1st quarter: 7th–13th.** Sow crops that develop below ground. Dig the soil.

**1st quarter to full moon: 13th–21st.** Sow crops that develop above ground. Plant seedlings and young plants.

**Full moon to 3rd quarter: 21st–29th.** Harvest crops for immediate eating. Harvest fruit.

## Moon sign – Virgo

Astrologers believe that the new moon is a time to make plans and focus on your dreams and hopes for the period ahead, and that each new moon has a particular energy, depending on which zodiacal sign it is in. The new moon on the 7th will be in Virgo, which is said to govern organisation and health, making this a good time to review administrative systems and to improve eating and exercise regimes.

*This month the full moon falls in the early hours of the morning. To see the moon at its fullest within normal waking hours, view it the evening before the date given above.

### Navigating by the stars, sun and moon

#### Use sun and moon rises and sets
This is barely a method, more a little basic solar and lunar knowledge that might help you get your bearing, particularly if you manage to see the sun or the moon rising or setting. First, know that the sun and moon follow roughly the same path across the sky: they rise in the east, track across the southern sky and set in the west. The exact point at which they rise and set changes through the year, though, by 40 degrees: it is only at the equinoxes in March and September that they rise and set due east and due west, and by midsummer the sun rises at almost northeast and at midwinter at almost southeast.

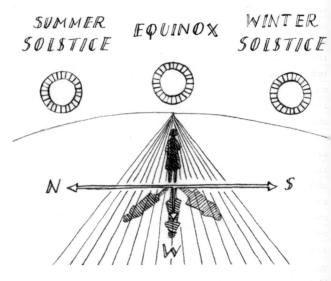

## Moon rise and set

| | *St Michael's Mount* | | *Hopton-on-Sea* | | |
|---|---|---|---|---|---|
| | Rise | Set | Rise | Set | |
| 1st | 00.10 | 17.22 | — | 17.08 | |
| 2nd | 00.56 | 18.13 | 00.11 | 17.58 | |
| 3rd | 01.54 | 18.54 | 01.09 | 18.37 | |
| 4th | 03.01 | 19.26 | 02.18 | 19.08 | |
| 5th | 04.15 | 19.52 | 03.34 | 19.31 | |
| 6th | 05.33 | 20.14 | 04.55 | 19.50 | |
| 7th | 06.52 | 20.32 | 06.17 | 20.06 | new moon |
| 8th | 08.12 | 20.50 | 07.40 | 20.21 | |
| 9th | 09.33 | 21.08 | 09.04 | 20.36 | |
| 10th | 10.55 | 21.27 | 10.29 | 20.53 | |
| 11th | 12.19 | 21.51 | 11.56 | 21.13 | |
| 12th | 13.43 | 22.20 | 13.24 | 21.39 | |
| 13th | 15.05 | 22.59 | 14.48 | 22.15 | 1st quarter |
| 14th | 16.18 | 23.50 | 16.04 | 23.04 | |
| 15th | 17.19 | — | 17.04 | — | |
| 16th | 18.05 | 00.55 | 17.49 | 00.09 | |
| 17th | 18.39 | 02.09 | 18.21 | 01.25 | |
| 18th | 19.05 | 03.27 | 18.44 | 02.47 | |
| 19th | 19.26 | 04.46 | 19.02 | 04.08 | |
| 20th | 19.43 | 06.02 | 19.17 | 05.27 | |
| 21st | 19.58 | 07.16 | 19.30 | 06.44 | full moon |
| 22nd | 20.13 | 08.28 | 19.42 | 07.58 | |
| 23rd | 20.29 | 09.38 | 19.55 | 09.11 | |
| 24th | 20.46 | 10.48 | 20.10 | 10.24 | |
| 25th | 21.07 | 11.57 | 20.28 | 11.36 | |
| 26th | 21.32 | 13.06 | 20.51 | 12.47 | |
| 27th | 22.04 | 14.12 | 21.21 | 13.56 | |
| 28th | 22.46 | 15.13 | 22.01 | 14.58 | |
| 29th | 23.38 | 16.06 | 22.53 | 15.52 | 3rd quarter |
| 30th | — | 16.50 | 23.56 | 16.35 | |

Where moonset times are before moonrise times, this is the setting of the previous night's moon.

# THE SKY

## At night

**10th:** Close approach of Venus and the moon, visible in the dusk from about 19.30 in the southwest at an altitude of 8 degrees, until setting at 20.30 in the southwest.

**16th:** Close approach of Saturn and the moon with Jupiter nearby, visible in the dusk from about 19.30 at 10 degrees altitude in the southeast, reaching a maximum altitude of 18 degrees in the south at 22.00 and setting at 01.30 in the southwest.

**18th:** Close approach of Jupiter and the moon, visible in the dusk from about 19.30, at an altitude of 10 degrees in the southeast, reaching a maximum altitude of 20 degrees in the south at 01.00 and setting at 02.30 in the southwest.

## By day

**1st:** Earliest sunrise, St Michael's Mount (06.36) and Hopton-on-Sea (06.04).

**1st:** Latest sunset, St Michael's Mount (20.05) and Hopton-on-Sea (19.40).

**1st–30th:** Daylight decreases by 1h 47m at St Michael's Mount and by 1h 57m at Hopton-on-Sea.

**21st:** At solar midday (approximately 13.00 BST/IST) the sun reaches an altitude of 40 degrees at Lee-on-the-Solent in Hampshire and 33 degrees at Lairg in Scotland.

**22nd:** The autumnal equinox falls at 19.21. (The equinox is the moment when the sun is directly over the equator. The word comes from the Latin *aequi*, or 'equal', and *nox*, or 'night'. Equinox occurs twice a year, in March and September.)

## Sunrise and set

|       | St Michael's Mount | | Hopton-on-Sea | |
|-------|-------|-------|-------|-------|
|       | Rise  | Set   | Rise  | Set   |
| 1st   | 06.36 | 20.05 | 06.04 | 19.40 |
| 2nd   | 06.38 | 20.03 | 06.05 | 19.38 |
| 3rd   | 06.39 | 20.01 | 06.07 | 19.36 |
| 4th   | 06.41 | 19.59 | 06.09 | 19.33 |
| 5th   | 06.42 | 19.57 | 06.10 | 19.31 |
| 6th   | 06.44 | 19.54 | 06.12 | 19.29 |
| 7th   | 06.45 | 19.52 | 06.14 | 19.26 |
| 8th   | 06.47 | 19.50 | 06.15 | 19.24 |
| 9th   | 06.48 | 19.48 | 06.17 | 19.22 |
| 10th  | 06.50 | 19.46 | 06.19 | 19.19 |
| 11th  | 06.51 | 19.43 | 06.20 | 19.17 |
| 12th  | 06.53 | 19.41 | 06.22 | 19.14 |
| 13th  | 06.54 | 19.39 | 06.24 | 19.12 |
| 14th  | 06.56 | 19.37 | 06.25 | 19.10 |
| 15th  | 06.57 | 19.35 | 06.27 | 19.07 |
| 16th  | 06.59 | 19.32 | 06.29 | 19.05 |
| 17th  | 07.00 | 19.30 | 06.30 | 19.03 |
| 18th  | 07.02 | 19.28 | 06.32 | 19.00 |
| 19th  | 07.03 | 19.26 | 06.34 | 18.58 |
| 20th  | 07.05 | 19.24 | 06.35 | 18.55 |
| 21st  | 07.06 | 19.21 | 06.37 | 18.53 |
| 22nd  | 07.08 | 19.19 | 06.39 | 18.51 |
| 23rd  | 07.09 | 19.17 | 06.40 | 18.48 |
| 24th  | 07.11 | 19.15 | 06.42 | 18.46 |
| 25th  | 07.12 | 19.13 | 06.44 | 18.44 |
| 26th  | 07.14 | 19.10 | 06.45 | 18.41 |
| 27th  | 07.15 | 19.08 | 06.47 | 18.39 |
| 28th  | 07.17 | 19.06 | 06.49 | 18.36 |
| 29th  | 07.19 | 19.04 | 06.50 | 18.34 |
| 30th  | 07.20 | 19.02 | 06.52 | 18.32 |

S

# THE SEA

### Average sea temperature

| | |
|---|---|
| Orkney: | 12.8°C |
| South Shields: | 14.8°C |
| Carrickfergus: | 14.2°C |
| Lowestoft: | 16.7°C |
| Aberystwyth: | 15.6°C |
| Bantry: | 15.6°C |
| Cowes: | 17.2°C |
| Penzance: | 16.3°C |

### Spring and neap tides

The spring tides are the most extreme tides of the month, with the highest rises and falls, and the neap tides are the least extreme, with the smallest. Exact timings vary around the coast, but expect them around the following dates:

**Spring tides:** 9th–10th and 22nd–23rd

**Neap tides:** 1st–2nd, 15th–16th and 30th

In the tide timetable opposite, spring tides are shown with an asterisk.

## September tide timetable for Dover

For guidance on how to convert this for your local area, see page 8.

|  | *High water* | | *Low water* | |
|---|---|---|---|---|
|  | Morning | Afternoon | Morning | Afternoon |
| 1st | 07.09 | 19.33 | 00.57 | 13.41 |
| 2nd | 08.22 | 20.45 | 02.39 | 15.18 |
| 3rd | 09.25 | 21.44 | 03.53 | 16.23 |
| 4th | 10.14 | 22.31 | 04.52 | 17.17 |
| 5th | 10.54 | 23.11 | 05.43 | 18.05 |
| 6th | 11.31 | 23.48 | 06.29 | 18.51 |
| 7th | — | 12.07 | 07.13 | 19.35 |
| 8th | 00.24 | 12.43 | 07.54 | 20.17 |
| 9th | 00.59 | 13.20 | 08.33 | 20.56 * |
| 10th | 01.35 | 13.58 | 09.08 | 21.32 * |
| 11th | 02.13 | 14.38 | 09.43 | 22.07 |
| 12th | 02.55 | 15.22 | 10.20 | 22.46 |
| 13th | 03.43 | 16.14 | 11.01 | 23.31 |
| 14th | 04.42 | 17.21 | 11.53 | — |
| 15th | 06.08 | 18.55 | 00.31 | 13.06 |
| 16th | 07.49 | 20.38 | 01.57 | 14.40 |
| 17th | 09.14 | 22.00 | 03.34 | 16.19 |
| 18th | 10.17 | 22.56 | 05.09 | 17.38 |
| 19th | 11.04 | 23.39 | 06.10 | 18.33 |
| 20th | 11.44 | — | 06.58 | 19.20 |
| 21st | 00.15 | 12.20 | 07.39 | 19.59 |
| 22nd | 00.46 | 12.55 | 08.13 | 20.33 * |
| 23rd | 01.16 | 13.30 | 08.41 | 20.59 * |
| 24th | 01.48 | 14.02 | 09.03 | 21.20 |
| 25th | 02.17 | 14.29 | 09.21 | 21.38 |
| 26th | 02.43 | 14.50 | 09.42 | 22.00 |
| 27th | 03.03 | 15.13 | 10.10 | 22.29 |
| 28th | 03.29 | 15.48 | 10.45 | 23.07 |
| 29th | 04.12 | 16.52 | 11.30 | 23.59 |
| 30th | 06.28 | 19.01 | — | 12.36 |

S

# A SEA SHANTY FOR SEPTEMBER

### Ek Dam!

Within Hinduism water is thought to activate luck and to cure problems, and this month for Ganesh Chaturthi – Ganesh's birthday – statues of the elephant god are carried in great processions to the sea and immersed. The most famous British example happens in Hounslow, west London, with Ganesh immersed in the River Thames. He is traditionally invoked before beginning journeys or new ventures.

To mark this, here is a rare example of a shanty in which Hindustani and pidgin English are mixed. Stan Hugill, in his book *Shanties from the Seven Seas*, says that he believes it would have originated among the lascars and khlassies, or Indian sailors, who worked the Nourse Line. These ships sailed from European ports, carrying a cargo of salt or steel to Calcutta. There they picked up indentured labourers and transported them to the Caribbean to carry out plantation work following the abolition of slavery in 1833. They then sailed up the American east coast and picked up grain, which they transported back to Europe.

Hugill knew the shanty as 'Eki-Duma' and thought this may be a corruption of the Hindustani expression *ek dom*, meaning 'one man', whereas the shanty singer Clint Hulton suggests that it comes from *ek-dam*, meaning 'one breath', or, effectively 'all together'. This was a halyard shanty, sung when hauling on a halyard (a rope, or line) to hoist a topsail, with the pull on the 'Ek'.

Kay kay kay kay! Ek Dam!
Kay kay kay kay! Ek Dam!

Sailorman no likee Bosun's Mate, *Ek Dam!*
Bosun's Mate no likee Head Serang, *Ek Dam!*
Head Serang no likee Number One, *Ek Dam!*
Number One no likee Khlassie Man, *Ek Dam!*

Kay kay kay kay! *Ek Dam!*
Kay kay kay kay! *Ek Dam!*

S

CARBIS BAY

KNILL'S MONUMENT

BOWL ROCK

LELANT

TRENCROM HILL

NINNES BRIDGE

LUDGVAN CHURCH

RED RIVER

MARAZION MARSH

MARAZION

ST MICHAEL'S MOUNT

· A MAP OF ·
ST MICHAEL'S WAY
· CORNWALL ·

# PILGRIMAGE OF THE MONTH

**St Michael's Way for Michaelmas**

The most famous European pilgrimage is the Camino de Santiago, a network of paths leading to the Catedral de Santiago de Compostela, Spain. The Cathedral is one of only three in the world built over the tomb of an apostle of Jesus, in this case St James the Great. The Camino, consisting of a network of pilgrims' ways, has been a major pilgrimage route since medieval times and has seen a great revival over the past decades, with the Camino Francés, through France and Spain, the most popular route. This has led surrounding countries to investigate how their own pilgrims would have travelled there, and to reinstate their own pilgrim paths.

One of the pilgrim routes in the Camino de Santiago network is the St Michael's Way, running roughly 20km from the north Cornish coast at Lelant to the south Cornish coast at Marazion, overlooking St Michael's Mount. Archaeology and old shipping records suggest that pilgrims travelling from Ireland and Wales to complete the Camino took this land route to avoid sailing the perilous waters around Land's End. St Michael's Way is a beautiful route in itself, and September, the month of Michaelmas, is a fine month to walk it. It works its way along country lanes and bridleways to Trencrom Hill, the site of an ancient hill fort and from where you can take in a panoramic view of both coasts and down towards Lands End, looking ahead to St Michael's Mount surrounded by glittering seas, and the end point of this particular leg of pilgrimage.

The paths of St Michael's Way are now waymarked by St James's scallop shell, just as those of the rest of the Camino are. It is now an official extension of the Camino Inglés, which runs approximately 75km from A Coruña in northern Spain to Santiago de Compostela. Historical evidence suggests that this is where ships of pilgrims would arrive from England. As pilgrims must walk at least 100km to receive a certificate of pilgrimage, they can now do so along the Camino Inglés if they first journey coast to coast across this narrow and beautiful slice of Cornwall towards St Michael's Mount.

S

# THE GARDEN

## September garden meditation

We have reached another tipping point. This month sees the autumnal equinox, the moment after which the nights will be longer than the days. Stand in the garden and think about how the spot in which you are standing is tipping away from the sun into the darker half of the year. Your garden knows it, and anticipates it. What has changed? Can you feel the nip in the air? A slight chill against your skin? Seeds are forming and falling to the earth to lie dormant through the long, cold months ahead, waiting for spring. Reproduction is being ensured everywhere you look, but so is survival. Know that hedgehogs, snuffling around your garden at night, are gorging on the bounty of the moment, fattening up for winter, and other small mammals are tucking away your berries and making cosy winter homes for themselves. Think about how your garden's role is about to change; it will soon become a haven and a refuge. Notice how most of your plants still appear to be soldiering on, but there is a change. They are no longer actively growing. All activity has been shifted now to ripening – of fruits, yes, but also of stems and leaves. Everything is starting to toughen up and shut down.

## Jobs in the garden

- Sow seeds of hardy annuals for cut flowers direct in your garden now. Cornflowers, calendula, larkspur and love-in-a-mist will all make bigger plants with more flowers if sown now.
- Buy vine weevil biological control and water it into all of your pots. These little unseen horrors can munch away on potted roots all winter.
- Plant daffodils. Choose miniature types and plant up several pots to position by your door next spring.

## How much to sow

It is tempting to sow whole packets of seeds and then be overwhelmed by seedlings or, later, great gluts of one type of vegetable. This guide will help you to sow roughly the amount you need for a family of four; adjust to suit your own circumstances and favourites. In every case, sow a small number more than suggested to allow for non-germination and seedling failure.

**Corn salad, rocket, spinach and spring onion:** Sow a 1-m row of each.

**Lettuce:** Sow a 3-m row of hardy winter lettuces, and perhaps 1m each of three different varieties.

**Oriental leaves:** Sow direct a 2-m row each of mizuna, mibuna, pak choi and red mustard.

S

# THE KITCHEN

### Romani recipe for September – Hazelnut bake

The hedgerows are full of hazelnuts just ready for harvesting and this is a recipe to use up a glut of them. Recipe based on the research of Romani and Traveller historian Robert Dawson.

Mash 450g cooked potatoes with a little milk and 450g shelled and crushed hazelnuts, a beaten egg and salt and pepper. Form into little balls and place on a well-greased baking tray, then cook in a Dutch oven over a medium heat, or bake in a moderate oven, until brown, basting with a little hot fat now and then.

### In season

### In the hedgerows, woods and fields
**Edible wild flowers:** Meadowsweet, nasturtium (flowers and seeds)
**Wild fruits and nuts:** Bilberry, blackberry, crab apple, elderberry, juniper berries, rosehips, rowan berries, damsons, haws, cobnuts, hazelnuts, walnuts
**Roots:** Alexanders, dandelion, horseradish, Jerusalem artichoke, lovage, rampion, wild garlic
**Game:** Hare, mallard, partridge, rabbit, grouse, ptarmigan, snipe, venison, wood pigeon

### From the seashore and rivers
**Fish and shellfish:** Eel, mussels, oysters, black bream, brown crab, herring, lobster, mackerel, turbot, scallops, hake, megrim sole, sardines, salmon
Sea buckthorn

**From the kitchen garden**
**Vegetables:** Tomatoes, aubergines, chillies, sweet peppers,
runner beans, French beans, peas, beetroot, calabrese, cabbages,
carrots, cauliflower, chard, courgettes, cucumber, endive, fennel,
garlic, kale, leeks, lettuce, onions, spring onions, shallots,
swede, sweetcorn, Oriental leaves, pumpkins, winter squash,
wild rocket, spinach, turnips
**Fruits and nuts:** Apples, pears, loganberries, autumn
raspberries, blackberries, plums, redcurrants, cobnuts
**Herbs:** Basil, mint, dill, oregano, thyme, marjoram

**From the farms**
Goose

S

# RECIPES

### Sugared damsons

This is a gorgeous way of preserving plums and was very popular in Victorian times, particularly for Christmas treats. It is a bit of a faff, but only because each stage of the process needs to be left alone for a spell of time: the actual 'doing' time is very minimal. This is adapted from a recipe in Adele Nozedar's *Hedgerow Handbook*.

| Makes up to 20 |
| --- |
| **Ingredients** |
| *For the syrup* |
| 250g caster sugar |
| A few fennel seeds |
| 500g damsons, washed, dried and with the stalks removed |
| |
| *To make the sugared damsons* |
| 500g caster sugar |

### Method
The first stage is to soak the damsons in syrup. Put 600ml water, the sugar and the fennel seeds in a pan and heat slowly until the sugar has dissolved. Bring to the boil and boil for a minute or so, then leave to cool. Put the damsons into a large sterilised jar and pour the syrup over them. Seal the jar and leave to soak for 3 months.

After that time, you can just eat the fruits with ice cream or cream, or you can continue on to the sugaring stage, in which case tip the damsons out of the jar into a colander placed over a bowl to catch the syrup. (Bottle this syrup for use on ice cream or in cocktails). Line a baking tray with greaseproof paper and tip the caster sugar onto a plate.

Now take a damson, roll it in the sugar, and lay it on the tray. Do the same with the rest, leave them for an hour or so, and then repeat the process.

Preheat the oven to the lowest possible temperature. Place the damsons in the oven for several hours, then remove them and repeat the double-rolling and baking again. You will need to do this 4 times altogether, which will take several days, but when finished the damsons will have a dry, crisp sugar coating and can be put into boxes to make beautiful gifts.

### Cheddar, apple and pickled onion focaccia

A harvest supper baked into a loaf. Apples, onions, a hunk of cheese and a loaf of bread would have been standard fare for those out in the fields bringing the harvests in, all easily transported foods that are delicious together. The pickers and gatherers would undoubtedly have made short work of this fancy version, too.

### Serves 4–6

### Ingredients

10g instant yeast

500g strong bread flour

1 teaspoon fine salt

2 tablespoons extra virgin olive oil, plus more for brushing and drizzling

1 crisp dessert apple, peeled, cored and cut into chunks

200g mature Cheddar cheese, cut into dice

6 pickled onions, quartered

1 teaspoon sea salt flakes

S

## Method

Tip 400ml warm water and the yeast into a bowl and stir together, then leave for 5 minutes until the top starts to foam. Add the flour, fine salt and the 2 tablespoons of olive oil, and stir to combine everything, then keep stirring to start the kneading process. You will have made a very wet dough, so knead it in the bowl for 5 minutes until it becomes less sticky, then turn it out onto an oiled surface and knead for 5 minutes more. Brush a clean bowl with olive oil, put the dough into it, cover with a tea towel and leave in a warm place to double in size, about 1– 1½ hours.

Brush a large baking tray liberally with olive oil, tip the dough onto it and then use your fingertips to push it towards the corners of the tray and flatten it. Cover with a large plastic bag, making sure it doesn't touch the dough, and leave to rise again for an hour.

Preheat the oven to 220°C/Gas Mark 7. Remove the focaccia from the bag and brush liberally all over with olive oil. Scatter the apple, Cheddar and pickled onion pieces over it, and push them lightly down into the dough, then sprinkle with the sea salt flakes. Bake for around 25 minutes or until golden. Remove from the oven and drizzle over a little more oil. Serve warm or cold.

# MIGRATION OF THE MONTH

### Nathusius' pipistrelle bat

The first hints that Nathusius' pipistrelle bats were making long autumnal migrations towards the UK and Ireland were when they started turning up on North Sea oil platforms, taking a breather from their mammoth journey, and then hurtling off again into the sea spray. These tiny bats, their bodies just 5–6cm in length, are this month heading our way for a cosy winter hibernation. Central and Eastern Europe, where the bats spend the summer feeding and breeding, have hard, cold winters and so some Nathusius' pipistrelles head south to Spain and Portugal for winter, while others head due west to enjoy the mild and soggy delights that Britain and Ireland can offer.

Their spring and summer in Poland, Lithuania and Latvia will have been spent in maternity roosts of up to 350 females, who emerge at dusk and fly through woodland treetops or over bodies of water, eating mosquitos and other flying insects. The males roost nearby and spend hours each night singing social calls to attract females for mating. From the end of July the babies are born, and each female will give birth to and raise a single bat, feeding it with her milk for about four weeks until it is able to fly and set about foraging for itself. By September the offspring are strong enough to join the migration west.

When the bats get here, they will be on the lookout for nooks and crannies: crevices in cliffs and caves, and tree holes, and they make great use of bat boxes. The bats will forage for flying insects, flitting through the treetops at woodland edges and near lakes to build themselves back up after their long flight, and then settle in for hibernation, before emerging and setting off across sea and land next spring.

S

OCTOBER

PUT A TENGER O

MONTH OF THE POTATOES

X

# October

 Start of Black History Month

 7th–14th: Navaratri – autumn festival (Hindu)

 Prophet Muhammad's birthday (Muslim) – celebrations begin the evening before

 Apple Day

 Stow Horse Fair – autumn Gypsy, Romani and Traveller gathering

 October bank holiday, Republic of Ireland

 British Summer Time and Irish Standard Time end. Clocks go back one hour at 02.00

 Hallowe'en

# ROMANI NAME FOR THE MONTH

## Putatengero – month of the potatoes

This was the final month of the big harvesting jobs for Romani families, and the 'tater picking up' was a big job to see them into the autumn. It was hard work, bending all day and then lifting the heavy loads of potatoes, but it was lucrative and carried out as the days turned increasingly cool and the leaves started to turn, the morning's fire suddenly particularly welcome to see off the night's chill and mists.

There is also a second and more controversial Welsh Romani name for October: Urchengero, month of the hedgehogs. Being marginalised from society, Romanies were forced either to live off wild things or to starve. It made them skilled trappers and hunters, making use of any wild food they could get hold of, catching rabbits and poaching pheasant for the pot. Although hedgehogs have been in severe decline over the last two decades and are now a protected species, until the mid-20th century they were abundant. They were seen by the Romani as just another form of wild food, and a particularly useful one at that. There are strict rules within Romani culture forbidding eating animals during their breeding season, when they are considered 'unclean', a rule that would also handily have allowed populations of the animals to replenish themselves. It was well understood that you only took a small number of any one creature, so that the balance of nature was not disturbed.

In October the breeding season was over and the hedgehogs had fattened themselves up and gone into their winter hibernation, and so were full of calories for hungry people working hard in increasingly cold conditions. After cooking, the legs were given to children to eat as snacks, and the lard was particularly prized to fry blackthorn thorns for preserving them as waterproof tent pins. During this month, early mushrooms, berries and wild roots such as dandelion, lovage and rampion were also all at their fattest.

# THE MOON

## Moon phases

New moon – 6th October, 12.05

1st quarter – 13th October, 04.25

Full moon – 20th October, 15.57

3rd quarter – 28th October, 21.05

## Gardening by the moon

**3rd quarter to new moon: 1st–6th and 28th–31st.** Prune. Harvest for storage. Fertilise and mulch the soil.

**New moon to 1st quarter: 6th–13th.** Sow crops that develop below ground. Dig the soil.

**1st quarter to full moon: 13th–20th.** Sow crops that develop above ground. Plant seedlings and young plants.

**Full moon to 3rd quarter: 20th–28th.** Harvest crops for immediate eating. Harvest fruit.

## Moon sign – Libra

Astrologers believe that the new moon is a time to make plans and focus on your dreams and hopes for the period ahead, and that each new moon has a particular energy, depending on which zodiacal sign it is in. The new moon on the 6th will be in Libra, which is said to govern negotiations and diplomacy, making this a good time to try to break long-standing deadlocks and to negotiate deals.

O

### Navigating by the stars, sun and moon

#### Find your direction from any star

You know how it is: you're out in the wilderness, hiking through the night, and your phone runs out of battery. You know there's a cosy cabin and some hot soup to the northwest, but which way is northwest? Never fear, for as long as it is a clear night you can use any bright star to work out your direction. Find two straight sticks, one about 15cm longer than the other, and then sit or crouch on the ground. Push the shorter stick into the ground just in front of you, then choose any bright star in the sky and line it up with the top of the stick and push the second, longer stick into the ground a little way behind the first stick so that the top of it lines up, too. This will set your star's position and you will be able to find it again as long as you return to roughly the same position. After five or ten minutes, check your homemade 'sight' again. If the star appears to have moved to the left you are facing north, or if to the right you are facing south. If it has risen you are looking east, and if it has sunk you are looking west.

## Moon rise and set

| | St Michael's Mount | | Hopton-on-Sea | | |
|---|---|---|---|---|---|
| | Rise | Set | Rise | Set | |
| 1st | 00.41 | 17.26 | — | 17.09 | |
| 2nd | 01.51 | 17.54 | 01.09 | 17.34 | |
| 3rd | 03.07 | 18.17 | 02.28 | 17.54 | |
| 4th | 04.26 | 18.36 | 03.50 | 18.11 | |
| 5th | 05.47 | 18.54 | 05.13 | 18.26 | |
| 6th | 07.08 | 19.12 | 06.38 | 18.41 | new moon |
| 7th | 08.32 | 19.30 | 08.05 | 18.57 | |
| 8th | 09.59 | 19.52 | 09.35 | 19.16 | |
| 9th | 11.26 | 20.20 | 11.06 | 19.40 | |
| 10th | 12.52 | 20.56 | 12.35 | 20.12 | |
| 11th | 14.11 | 21.44 | 13.56 | 20.58 | |
| 12th | 15.16 | 22.45 | 15.03 | 21.59 | |
| 13th | 16.07 | 23.57 | 15.52 | 23.13 | 1st quarter |
| 14th | 16.44 | — | 16.27 | — | |
| 15th | 17.11 | 01.15 | 16.51 | 00.33 | |
| 16th | 17.33 | 02.33 | 17.10 | 01.54 | |
| 17th | 17.50 | 03.49 | 17.25 | 03.13 | |
| 18th | 18.05 | 05.02 | 17.38 | 04.29 | |
| 19th | 18.20 | 06.14 | 17.50 | 05.43 | |
| 20th | 18.35 | 07.24 | 18.02 | 06.56 | full moon |
| 21st | 18.51 | 08.34 | 18.16 | 08.09 | |
| 22nd | 19.10 | 09.43 | 18.32 | 09.21 | |
| 23rd | 19.33 | 10.53 | 18.53 | 10.33 | |
| 24th | 20.02 | 12.00 | 19.19 | 11.44 | |
| 25th | 20.40 | 13.04 | 19.55 | 12.49 | |
| 26th | 21.27 | 14.00 | 20.41 | 13.46 | |
| 27th | 22.25 | 14.48 | 21.40 | 14.33 | |
| 28th | 23.31 | 15.25 | 22.48 | 15.09 | 3rd quarter |
| 29th | — | 15.55 | — | 15.37 | |
| 30th | 00.44 | 16.19 | 00.03 | 15.58 | |
| 31st | 01.00 | 15.39 | 01.22 | 15.16 | |

Where moonset times are before moonrise times, this is the setting of the previous night's moon.
British Summer Time and Irish Standard Time end on 31st October at 02.00, and this has been accounted for above.

# THE SKY

## At night

**14th:** Close approach of Saturn and the moon, visible in the dusk from about 18.30 at 14 degrees altitude in the southeast, reaching a maximum altitude of 17 degrees in the south at 20.30 and setting at 00.00 in the southwest.

**15th:** Close approach of Jupiter and the moon, visible in the dusk from about 18.30, at an altitude of 12 degrees in the southeast, reaching a maximum altitude of 21 degrees in the south at 21.00 and setting at 01.30 in the southwest.

## By day

**1st:** At solar midday (approximately 13.00 BST/IST) the sun reaches an altitude of 28 degrees at Lee-on-the-Solent in Hampshire and 21 degrees at Lairg in Scotland.

**1st:** Earliest sunrise, St Michael's Mount (07.22) and Hopton-on-Sea (06.54).

**1st:** Latest sunset, St Michael's Mount (18.59) and Hopton-on-Sea (18.29).

**1st–31st:** Daylight decreases by 1h 48m at St Michael's Mount and by 1h 59m at Hopton-on-Sea.

## Sunrise and set

| | St Michael's Mount | | Hopton-on-Sea | |
|---|---|---|---|---|
| | Rise | Set | Rise | Set |
| 1st | 07.22 | 18.59 | 06.54 | 18.29 |
| 2nd | 07.23 | 18.57 | 06.56 | 18.27 |
| 3rd | 07.25 | 18.55 | 06.57 | 18.25 |
| 4th | 07.26 | 18.53 | 06.59 | 18.22 |
| 5th | 07.28 | 18.51 | 07.01 | 18.20 |
| 6th | 07.29 | 18.49 | 07.03 | 18.18 |
| 7th | 07.31 | 18.46 | 07.04 | 18.15 |
| 8th | 07.33 | 18.44 | 07.06 | 18.13 |
| 9th | 07.34 | 18.42 | 07.08 | 18.11 |
| 10th | 07.36 | 18.40 | 07.09 | 18.09 |
| 11th | 07.37 | 18.38 | 07.11 | 18.06 |
| 12th | 07.39 | 18.36 | 07.13 | 18.04 |
| 13th | 07.40 | 18.34 | 07.15 | 18.02 |
| 14th | 07.42 | 18.32 | 07.17 | 18.00 |
| 15th | 07.44 | 18.30 | 07.18 | 17.57 |
| 16th | 07.45 | 18.28 | 07.20 | 17.55 |
| 17th | 07.47 | 18.26 | 07.22 | 17.53 |
| 18th | 07.48 | 18.24 | 07.24 | 17.51 |
| 19th | 07.50 | 18.22 | 07.25 | 17.49 |
| 20th | 07.52 | 18.20 | 07.27 | 17.47 |
| 21st | 07.53 | 18.18 | 07.29 | 17.44 |
| 22nd | 07.55 | 18.16 | 07.31 | 17.42 |
| 23rd | 07.57 | 18.14 | 07.33 | 17.40 |
| 24th | 07.58 | 18.12 | 07.34 | 17.38 |
| 25th | 08.00 | 18.10 | 07.36 | 17.36 |
| 26th | 08.02 | 18.08 | 07.38 | 17.34 |
| 27th | 08.03 | 18.06 | 07.40 | 17.32 |
| 28th | 08.05 | 18.05 | 07.42 | 17.30 |
| 29th | 08.07 | 18.03 | 07.44 | 17.28 |
| 30th | 08.08 | 18.01 | 07.45 | 17.26 |
| 31st | 07.10 | 16.59 | 06.47 | 16.24 |

British Summer Time and Irish Standard Time end on 31st October at 02.00, and this has been accounted for above.

# THE SEA

## Average sea temperature

| | |
|---|---|
| Orkney: | 12°C |
| South Shields: | 12.9°C |
| Carrickfergus: | 13.4°C |
| Lowestoft: | 15.1°C |
| Aberystwyth: | 14.5°C |
| Bantry: | 14.1°C |
| Cowes: | 16.2°C |
| Penzance: | 14.8°C |

## Spring and neap tides

The spring tides are the most extreme tides of the month, with the highest rises and falls, and the neap tides are the least extreme, with the smallest. Exact timings vary around the coast, but expect them around the following dates:

**Spring tides:** 8th–9th and 21st–22nd

**Neap tides:** 1st, 14th–15th and 29th–30th

In the tide timetable opposite, spring tides are shown with an asterisk.

## October tide timetable for Dover

For guidance on how to convert this for your local area, see page 8.

|        | High water |           | Low water |             |
|        | Morning    | Afternoon | Morning   | Afternoon   |
|--------|------------|-----------|-----------|-------------|
| 1st    | 07.45      | 20.14     | 01.47     | 14.39       |
| 2nd    | 08.49      | 21.14     | 03.22     | 15.52       |
| 3rd    | 09.40      | 22.01     | 04.24     | 16.47       |
| 4th    | 10.22      | 22.42     | 05.15     | 17.36       |
| 5th    | 11.00      | 23.20     | 06.02     | 18.23       |
| 6th    | 11.38      | 23.56     | 06.46     | 19.08       |
| 7th    | —          | 12.15     | 07.27     | 19.51       |
| 8th    | 00.33      | 12.53     | 08.06     | 20.31 *     |
| 9th    | 01.10      | 13.33     | 08.44     | 21.08 *     |
| 10th   | 01.51      | 14.15     | 09.21     | 21.45       |
| 11th   | 02.35      | 15.02     | 10.01     | 22.26       |
| 12th   | 03.26      | 15.58     | 10.45     | 23.13       |
| 13th   | 04.31      | 17.13     | 11.40     | —           |
| 14th   | 05.55      | 18.49     | 00.17     | 12.58       |
| 15th   | 07.31      | 20.36     | 01.50     | 14.39       |
| 16th   | 08.57      | 21.48     | 03.34     | 16.16       |
| 17th   | 09.57      | 22.38     | 04.53     | 17.21       |
| 18th   | 10.41      | 23.16     | 05.46     | 18.11       |
| 19th   | 11.19      | 23.48     | 06.30     | 18.53       |
| 20th   | 11.54      | —         | 07.07     | 19.29       |
| 21st   | 00.18      | 12.28     | 07.39     | 19.57 *     |
| 22nd   | 00.48      | 13.01     | 08.05     | 20.20 *     |
| 23rd   | 01.18      | 13.31     | 08.25     | 20.39       |
| 24th   | 01.46      | 13.54     | 08.46     | 21.01       |
| 25th   | 02.07      | 14.11     | 09.12     | 21.27       |
| 26th   | 02.25      | 14.36     | 09.43     | 21.59       |
| 27th   | 02.54      | 15.12     | 10.19     | 22.37       |
| 28th   | 03.37      | 16.05     | 11.02     | 23.25       |
| 29th   | 05.14      | 18.26     | —         | 12.01       |
| 30th   | 07.02      | 19.40     | 00.39     | 13.48       |
| 31st   | 07.07      | 19.39     | 01.38     | 14.11       |

British Summer Time and Irish Standard Time end on 31st October at 02.00, and this has been accounted for above.

O

# A SEA SHANTY FOR OCTOBER

**Roll the Cotton Down**

A shanty to mark Black History Month, which has been observed in the United Kingdom since 1987. As Stan Hugill states in his book *Shanties of the Seven Seas*, a great number of shanties have clear origins as the working songs of slaves on plantations in the American South and the West Indies. Indeed, the very notion of singing while working was an intrinsic part of African culture.

In the Southern port city of Mobile, Alabama, African American slaves – and, later, former slaves – worked packing the cotton onto ships bound for Europe, a hugely physical and demanding job. They were often joined in this work by English and Irish sailors, who sometimes overwintered in Mobile to avoid sailing during the treacherous North Atlantic winter. The African Americans sang songs as they worked, and these songs were picked up by the European sailors, sometimes in their entirety but often as fragments with their own words added later. There was a great flourishing of musical cross-pollination, with a particular wealth of Irish and African American crossovers, such as the words of an Irish song being set to the tune of an African American one. All was tumbled about in the great musical melting pot that was the Atlantic Ocean between 1815 and 1860, the age of merchant sailing ships and of sea shanties.

This shanty is pretty clearly of African American origin. It is a t'gallant halyard shanty, used when hauling the t'gallant halyard (rope, or line) to set the topgallant sail. The job needed a lively, quick beat, which this song provides if sung at a marching pace.

♩ = 60

Oh, way down south where I was born *Roll the cot-ton down!* Oh, I worked in the cot-ton and I worked in the corn *We'll roll the cot-ton down!* Roll the cot-ton! Roll the cot-ton, Mo-ses! Roll the cot-ton! We'll roll the cot-ton down!

Around Cape Horn we're bound to go
*Roll the cotton down!*
Around Cape Stiff through ice and snow
*We'll roll the cotton down!*
Roll the cotton!
*Roll the cotton, Moses!*
Roll the cotton!
*We'll roll the cotton down!*

We're bound away at the break of day
*Roll the cotton down!*
And come back here to Mobile Bay
*We'll roll the cotton down!...*

Oh, Mobile Bay's no place for me
*Roll the cotton down!*
I'll sail away on some other sea
*We'll roll the cotton down!...*

O

A MAP OF EUROPEAN EEL MIGRATION

# MIGRATION OF THE MONTH

**European eel**

This month hundreds of thousands of eels that have lived in our rivers and estuaries for up to 14 years will leave us, never to return. They will clamber across mud and even damp grassland, shake off silt, and slip downstream, heading towards the Atlantic Ocean. The eels' migration pattern is complex and mysterious, with several phases of it still only guessed at. Life seems to begin for them 5,000km away in the Sargasso Sea, an area of the western Atlantic Ocean northeast of Cuba, and the only named sea bounded by currents rather than land. It has an abundance of sargassum seaweed, and it is here that mature eels are thought to spawn larvae (though no one has ever seen it).

The larvae then drift on the Gulf Stream for up to three years, growing as they go, until they reach the coasts of Western Europe. At this point, in the first of several name changes, they are known as glass eels, because of their near-transparent bodies. The glass eels start to make their way inland up rivers, streams and even tiny creeks, piling on top of each other in their thousands at times to overcome obstacles and work their way far, far upstream. When in fresh water, they develop pigment, and at this stage they are known as elvers, or juvenile eels. They will live out their lives eating worms, insects and crustaceans until the time comes for their return (at which point they are known as yellow eels, for their golden pigmentation). At some mystery signal they up and leave.

Their return is not straightforward. For a start they don't take the most direct route across the Atlantic. Instead, they veer far south, presumably to catch the Gulf Stream current and hitch a ride back up to the Sargasso. And as they travel, their bodies change. Their guts dissolve, which means they must make the entire journey on stored energy, and their eyes enlarge, so that they can see through the murky ocean depths. Their bodies turn silvery (you guessed it: they are now called silver eels) so that they are harder to spot by predators. Once they have spawned in the Sargasso Sea, they will die, but not before sending a new generation of tiny larvae bobbing slowly towards us again on the ocean currents.

# THE GARDEN

### October garden meditation

Now the garden is swinging fully into autumn, there is no ignoring it. If you have been removing your shoes and socks for these garden meditations, you may feel a little more reluctant now. But do it anyway, particularly because there should still be some warmth held in the soil, stored up from the past summer of sunshine, and it is good to feel that for yourself. Look for the dew in the mornings, a sign that the air is cooling during the suddenly longer, colder nights, leaving the humidity in the air unable to suspend itself, and so settling on every leaf and spider's web. Note how the webs have suddenly started to proliferate, and imagine the spiders spinning their silken creations each night, ready to ensnare a fly or passing gardener the next morning.

There is a big change in the plants now, as they start to pull back in on themselves. Some are dying, but only after they have enthusiastically shed their seed. Others are dying back, but that is a different thing. Think about how they are pulling all of their energies into themselves, protecting themselves from what is to come. With some plants this means retreating back under the ground, leaving all top parts to die; for others it means shedding leaves, leaving exposed only tough and gnarled trunks and stems. Look around your garden and think about this process beginning, and note all of the accidental beauty that it creates.

## Jobs in the garden

- Plant the edges of your lawn with spring bulbs: crocuses, tiny daffodils and species tulips.
- Anything tender needs to come inside now or be wrapped up. Move pelargoniums indoors or into glasshouses, wrap hardy bananas, and lift cannas and dahlias, storing them somewhere dry and frost-free.
- This is a great time to plant new hedging, whether evergreen and formal such as box, or deciduous, rustic and native to encourage wildlife.

## How much to sow

It is tempting to sow whole packets of seeds and then be overwhelmed by seedlings or, later, great gluts of one type of vegetable. This guide will help you to sow roughly the amount you need for a family of four; adjust to suit your own circumstances and favourites. In every case, sow a small number more than suggested to allow for non-germination and seedling failure.

**Broad beans:** Sow two 3-m rows direct into the ground.

**Garlic:** Plant one bulb of each of three varieties (they should contain up to ten cloves each).

**Lettuce:** You can still sow a few hardy lettuces if you have a sheltered place under cover.

O

# THE KITCHEN

### Romani recipe for October – Shushi stew

*Shushi* is the Romani name for rabbit. A stew such as this that could bubble gently away over a fire would be the most common meal for most families, particularly during the cold months. Recipe based on the research of Romani and Traveller historian Robert Dawson.

Cut 1 gutted and skinned rabbit into pieces and cook slowly in water or beer with some sliced onions until the meat is tender – about 2–2 ½ hours. Allow to cool and then carefully remove the bones and chop up any larger pieces of meat. Add 2 large sliced potatoes, 2 sliced carrots, some mushrooms, rosemary, salt and pepper and a large spoon of butter, then cook slowly over a low heat until the vegetables are cooked, about 20 minutes. Towards the end of cooking, you could add some 'swimmers', or 'dough boys' – soft, floury dumplings made from 150g self-raising flour, 70g suet, half a finely chopped onion, salt and pepper, and enough water to form a dough. Place them into the top of the dish and cook for about 20 minutes or until risen and soft.

## In season

### In the hedgerows, woods and fields
**Wild greens:** Chickweed, hairy bittercress, dandelion leaves, sow thistle, wintercress, sorrel
**Wild fruits and nuts:** Bullace, crab apple, elderberry, haws, juniper berries, rose, rowan berries, sloes, hazelnuts, sweet chestnuts, walnuts, wild damson
**Fungi:** Ceps, chanterelles, field mushrooms, horse mushrooms, common puffballs, parasols, shaggy inkcaps
**Roots:** Alexanders, dandelion, horseradish, Jerusalem artichoke, lovage, rampion, wild garlic
**Game:** Pheasant, grouse, woodcock, goose, hare, mallard, partridge, ptarmigan, rabbit, snipe, venison

### From the seashore and rivers
**Fish and shellfish:** Black bream, herring, lobster, mackerel, turbot, eels, oysters, hake, lemon sole, sardines
Sea buckthorn

### From the kitchen garden
**Vegetables:** Aubergines, chillies, sweet peppers, beetroot, Brussels sprouts, cabbages, carrots, cauliflower, celeriac, celery, chard, chicory, endive, fennel, garlic, Jerusalem artichokes, kale, leeks, lettuce, onions, spring onions, Oriental leaves, parsnips, potatoes, salsify, scorzonera, spinach, swede, tomatoes, turnips
**Fruits:** Medlars, quince, apples, pears
**Herbs:** Rosemary, sage, parsley, coriander, chervil

### And traditional imports
Truffles, Vacherin Mont d'Or

O

# RECIPES

### Sweet chestnut, walnut and tahini brownies

A brownie full of autumnal textures and flavours. Tahini makes a delicious addition to brownies, nutty and creamy, and adds a beautiful sepia swirl.

| Makes 24 |
| --- |
| **Ingredients** |
| 375g butter |
| 375g dark chocolate, broken into pieces |
| 6 eggs |
| 500g caster sugar |
| Seeds of 1 vanilla pod |
| 225g plain flour |
| Pinch of salt |
| 200g cooked and shelled chestnuts, roughly chopped |
| 200g walnuts, toasted in the oven for about 12 minutes, then roughly chopped |
| 3 tablespoons light tahini |

### Method

Line a baking tin with parchment and preheat the oven to 180°C/ Gas Mark 4. Put the butter and chocolate into a large bowl and set it over a pan of boiling water until they have melted. Put some cold water in a basin and carefully sit the bowl in it for a few minutes to cool, stirring the mixture occasionally.

Beat the eggs, sugar and vanilla together and then beat them into the cooled chocolate mixture. Stir in the flour, salt, chestnuts and walnuts. Pour the mixture onto the baking tray and smooth over the top. Blob the tahini onto the top and use the spoon or a knife to make swirls. Bake for about 35–40 minutes, or until the wobble is minimal and the top has started to crack. Remove, leave to cool completely, then cut into 24 squares and serve.

# PILGRIMAGE OF THE MONTH

**Trick-or-treating**

Trick-or-treating is a ritual journey passed down through the ages, albeit a pretty short journey that is mostly about fun and sweets. On Hallowe'en we dress up and parade around our neighbourhoods, a small and spooky annual pilgrimage.

The 31st October has always been associated with the supernatural, though it is unclear exactly why. We know that the 1st November was the festival of Samhain and was considered the first day of winter, and so on the 31st October, end-of-summer feasts and celebrations were held throughout Britain and Ireland. Such shifts from one season to the next have always been considered the times when fairies, goblins, trolls and witches were at their most active. In addition, the coldest, darkest times of the year were approaching, and hence the time of year likely to see the most deaths, and the countryside around reflected this in dying back and withering. Divination rituals – mainly revolving around who was going to die next – were a major part of Samhain Eve celebrations, perhaps because of this. All of these elements may have fed into the night's spooky associations, when it was thought pertinent to avoid churchyards and crossroads, places where spooks would be most likely to gather.

The origins of trick-or-treating itself lie in the far north of Scotland and in Ireland, where Samhain Eve was sometimes known as Puca Night, or Goblin Night. The practice of dressing up and parading, holding carved vegetable lamps, originated with mummers, players who would perform for winter festivals. Mimicking the very ghouls that everyone was scared of and parading around the neighbourhood was thought to scare them away. Following mass Irish emigration during Victorian times, the practice began to spread throughout Scotland, Wales and northern England and, of course, into America. From there it was imported – pumpkins and all – back to Britain and Ireland via popular culture.

O

NOVEMBER

MONTH OF THE SALMON

BARE-MACHENGERO

XI

# November

**1**   Samhain, end of harvest/beginning of winter celebration (Gaelic/pagan/neopagan)

**1**   All Saints' Day (Christian)

**2**   All Souls' Day (Christian)

**4**   Diwali – festival of lights (Hindu/Sikh/Jain)

**5**   Guy Fawkes Night

**6**   Bridgwater Carnival

**11**   Armistice Day/Remembrance Day

**11**   Martinmas (Christian, traditional)

**14**   Remembrance Sunday

**18**   Beaujolais Nouveau Day

**21**   Stir-up Sunday

**25**   Thanksgiving (American)

**28**   First Sunday in Advent (Christian)

**29**   29th November–6th December: Hanukkah – festival of lights (Jewish) – begins at sunset on 28th

**30**   St Andrew's Day, patron saint of Scotland

# ROMANI NAME FOR THE MONTH

## Bare-machengero – month of the salmon

For Welsh Romani and Scottish Travellers, this month held a special wild harvest, so good and abundant that the month was named after it. As the rivers were running with salmon, salmon poaching would be commonplace in November, with the fishing done by moonlight or in out-of-the-way corners of rivers to avoid gamekeepers. This was a wonderful source of nutritious wild food packed with protein and good, healthy fats. The Welsh Romanies in particular have always been good fishermen, and would fish Bala Lake in Snowdonia for pike, perch, brown trout, roach and eel. All would be brought back to the fire to be cooked and shared among the family and anyone else who came by, making a rare quick meal to replace the usual slow-cooked stews.

By November the farmers' harvests would all be in, but there was the wild harvest of sloes, hips and mushrooms to be foraged and eaten, and winter greens such as wintercress, chickweed and hairy bittercress to gather from the hedgerow bases. For most Romani families this was the time to start travelling to their winter stopping places, to put down temporary roots for the winter. If there were quiet times the women and children might set about making some of their traditional crafts to be sold in markets or door to door in nearby towns. They would gather hazel twigs and fashion them into clothes pegs, bound with strips of old tins to stop them splitting, and make beautiful roses curled from rolls of crepe paper and then dipped into wax. Selling these would keep money coming in during the leaner days after the major agricultural jobs had finished, and as winter was coming.

# THE MOON

## Moon phases

New moon – 4th November, 21.15

1st quarter – 11th November, 12.46

Full moon – 19th November, 08.57

3rd quarter – 27th November, 12.28

## Gardening by the moon

3rd quarter to new moon: 1st–4th and 27th–30th. Prune. Harvest for storage. Fertilise and mulch the soil.

New moon to 1st quarter: 4th–11th. Sow crops that develop below ground. Dig the soil.

1st quarter to full moon: 11th–19th. Sow crops that develop above ground. Plant seedlings and young plants.

Full moon to 3rd quarter: 19th–27th. Harvest crops for immediate eating. Harvest fruit.

## Moon sign – Scorpio

Astrologers believe that the new moon is a time to make plans and focus on your dreams and hopes for the period ahead, and that each new moon has a particular energy, depending on which zodiacal sign it is in. The new moon on the 4th will be in Scorpio, which is said to govern personal empowerment and desire, making this a good time to work on self-esteem and to deepen relationships.

N

**Navigating by the stars, sun and moon**

### Find south using Orion

Orion is one of our best-loved winter constellations. Vanishing below the horizon in early summer and reappearing in late summer, it becomes higher and more visible as winter deepens, riding high and bright in the sky all winter long. It is an easily recognised constellation and a particularly useful one for finding south. If you picture the constellation as a man – Orion the hunter, as he is known – you will see that as he moves from east to west through the sky he changes position, starting off leaning left, moving to upright, and then leaning right. Hanging from the belt of three bright stars at his waist is a 'sword' of three fainter stars, and it is this sword that is our navigational pointer. When Orion is upright and the sword is pointing directly downwards, it is pointing due south.

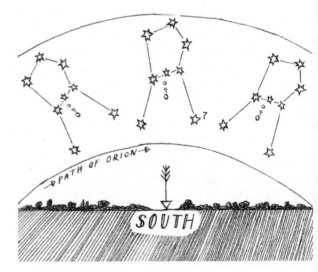

## Moon rise and set

| | St Michael's Mount | | Hopton-on-Sea | | |
|------|------|------|------|------|------|
| | Rise | Set | Rise | Set | |
| 1st | 02.18 | 15.57 | 01.43 | 15.31 | |
| 2nd | 03.38 | 16.14 | 03.06 | 15.45 | |
| 3rd | 05.00 | 16.32 | 04.31 | 16.00 | |
| 4th | 06.26 | 16.53 | 06.01 | 16.17 | new moon |
| 5th | 07.55 | 17.17 | 07.33 | 16.39 | |
| 6th | 09.26 | 17.50 | 09.07 | 17.08 | |
| 7th | 10.52 | 18.34 | 10.36 | 17.49 | |
| 8th | 12.06 | 19.32 | 11.53 | 18.46 | |
| 9th | 13.04 | 20.43 | 12.50 | 19.58 | |
| 10th | 13.47 | 22.02 | 13.30 | 21.19 | |
| 11th | 14.17 | 23.21 | 13.58 | 22.41 | 1st quarter |
| 12th | 14.40 | — | 14.18 | — | |
| 13th | 14.58 | 00.38 | 14.34 | 00.01 | |
| 14th | 15.14 | 01.52 | 14.47 | 01.18 | |
| 15th | 15.28 | 03.03 | 14.59 | 02.32 | |
| 16th | 15.43 | 04.13 | 15.11 | 03.45 | |
| 17th | 15.58 | 05.22 | 15.24 | 04.57 | |
| 18th | 16.16 | 06.32 | 15.39 | 06.09 | |
| 19th | 16.37 | 07.41 | 15.57 | 07.21 | full moon |
| 20th | 17.03 | 08.50 | 16.21 | 08.32 | |
| 21st | 17.38 | 09.55 | 16.53 | 09.40 | |
| 22nd | 18.22 | 10.55 | 17.36 | 10.40 | |
| 23rd | 19.16 | 11.45 | 18.30 | 11.31 | |
| 24th | 20.19 | 12.26 | 19.34 | 12.11 | |
| 25th | 21.28 | 12.58 | 20.46 | 12.40 | |
| 26th | 22.40 | 13.23 | 22.01 | 13.03 | |
| 27th | 23.55 | 13.44 | 23.19 | 13.21 | 3rd quarter |
| 28th | — | 14.02 | — | 13.37 | |
| 29th | 01.12 | 14.18 | 00.38 | 13.50 | |
| 30th | 02.30 | 14.35 | 02.00 | 14.04 | |

Where moonset times are before moonrise times, this is the setting of the previous night's moon.

# THE SKY

## At night

**10th:** Close approach of Saturn and the moon, visible in the dusk from about 16.30 at an altitude of 16 degrees in the south, until setting in the southwest at 21.00.

**11th:** Close approach of Jupiter and the moon, visible in the dusk from around 16.30, at an altitude of 16 degrees in the southeast, reaching a maximum altitude of 21 degrees in the south at 18.00 and setting at 22.30 in the southwest.

## By day

**1st:** At solar midday the sun reaches an altitude of 19 degrees at Lee-on-the-Solent in Hampshire and 12 degrees at Lairg in Scotland.

**1st:** Earliest sunrise, St Michael's Mount (07.12) and Hopton-on-Sea (06.49).

**1st:** Latest sunset, St Michael's Mount (16.58) and Hopton-on-Sea (16.22).

**1st–30th:** Daylight decreases by 1h 22m at St Michael's Mount and by 1h 30m at Hopton-on-Sea.

## Sunrise and set

| | St Michael's Mount | | Hopton-on-Sea | |
|---|---|---|---|---|
| | Rise | Set | Rise | Set |
| 1st | 07.12 | 16.58 | 06.49 | 16.22 |
| 2nd | 07.13 | 16.56 | 06.51 | 16.21 |
| 3rd | 07.15 | 16.54 | 06.53 | 16.19 |
| 4th | 07.17 | 16.53 | 06.55 | 16.17 |
| 5th | 07.18 | 16.51 | 06.56 | 16.15 |
| 6th | 07.20 | 16.49 | 06.58 | 16.13 |
| 7th | 07.22 | 16.48 | 07.00 | 16.12 |
| 8th | 07.23 | 16.46 | 07.02 | 16.10 |
| 9th | 07.25 | 16.45 | 07.04 | 16.08 |
| 10th | 07.27 | 16.43 | 07.06 | 16.07 |
| 11th | 07.28 | 16.42 | 07.07 | 16.05 |
| 12th | 07.30 | 16.41 | 07.09 | 16.04 |
| 13th | 07.32 | 16.39 | 07.11 | 16.02 |
| 14th | 07.33 | 16.38 | 07.13 | 16.01 |
| 15th | 07.35 | 16.37 | 07.15 | 15.59 |
| 16th | 07.36 | 16.35 | 07.16 | 15.58 |
| 17th | 07.38 | 16.34 | 07.18 | 15.56 |
| 18th | 07.40 | 16.33 | 07.20 | 15.55 |
| 19th | 07.41 | 16.32 | 07.22 | 15.54 |
| 20th | 07.43 | 16.31 | 07.23 | 15.53 |
| 21st | 07.44 | 16.30 | 07.25 | 15.51 |
| 22nd | 07.46 | 16.29 | 07.27 | 15.50 |
| 23rd | 07.47 | 16.28 | 07.28 | 15.49 |
| 24th | 07.49 | 16.27 | 07.30 | 15.48 |
| 25th | 07.50 | 16.26 | 07.32 | 15.47 |
| 26th | 07.52 | 16.25 | 07.33 | 15.46 |
| 27th | 07.53 | 16.24 | 07.35 | 15.45 |
| 28th | 07.55 | 16.24 | 07.36 | 15.44 |
| 29th | 07.56 | 16.23 | 07.38 | 15.44 |
| 30th | 07.57 | 16.22 | 07.39 | 15.43 |

N

# THE SEA

## Average sea temperature

| | |
|---|---:|
| Orkney: | 10.9°C |
| South Shields: | 11.1°C |
| Carrickfergus: | 12.3°C |
| Lowestoft: | 12.8°C |
| Aberystwyth: | 13°C |
| Bantry: | 12.7°C |
| Cowes: | 14.3°C |
| Penzance: | 13.3°C |

## Spring and neap tides

The spring tides are the most extreme tides of the month, with the highest rises and falls, and the neap tides are the least extreme, with the smallest. Exact timings vary around the coast, but expect them around the following dates:

**Spring tides:** 6th–7th and 20th–21st

**Neap tides:** 12th–13th and 27th–28th

In the tide timetable opposite, spring tides are shown with an asterisk.

## November tide timetable for Dover

For guidance on how to convert this for your local area, see page 8.

|       | High water | | Low water | |
|       | Morning | Afternoon | Morning | Afternoon |
|-------|---------|-----------|---------|-----------|
| 1st   | 08.01   | 20.27     | 02.45   | 15.09     |
| 2nd   | 08.46   | 21.10     | 03.39   | 16.01     |
| 3rd   | 09.27   | 21.49     | 04.28   | 16.51     |
| 4th   | 10.07   | 22.28     | 05.14   | 17.38     |
| 5th   | 10.47   | 23.08     | 05.59   | 18.24     |
| 6th   | 11.29   | 23.49     | 06.42   | 19.07 *   |
| 7th   | —       | 12.12     | 07.24   | 19.49 *   |
| 8th   | 00.33   | 12.58     | 08.06   | 20.30     |
| 9th   | 01.22   | 13.49     | 08.50   | 21.14     |
| 10th  | 02.17   | 14.51     | 09.39   | 22.05     |
| 11th  | 03.21   | 16.03     | 10.38   | 23.12     |
| 12th  | 04.33   | 17.31     | 11.54   | —         |
| 13th  | 05.56   | 19.08     | 00.36   | 13.21     |
| 14th  | 07.20   | 20.17     | 02.00   | 14.42     |
| 15th  | 08.21   | 21.05     | 03.11   | 15.45     |
| 16th  | 09.08   | 21.43     | 04.06   | 16.35     |
| 17th  | 09.48   | 22.17     | 04.51   | 17.17     |
| 18th  | 10.26   | 22.49     | 05.29   | 17.51     |
| 19th  | 11.01   | 23.20     | 06.02   | 18.19     |
| 20th  | 11.34   | 23.52     | 06.30   | 18.44 *   |
| 21st  | —       | 12.04     | 06.55   | 19.09 *   |
| 22nd  | 00.21   | 12.29     | 07.22   | 19.36     |
| 23rd  | 00.45   | 12.51     | 07.52   | 20.07     |
| 24th  | 01.08   | 13.18     | 08.26   | 20.40     |
| 25th  | 01.40   | 13.56     | 09.03   | 21.19     |
| 26th  | 02.23   | 14.47     | 09.46   | 22.04     |
| 27th  | 03.25   | 16.17     | 10.40   | 23.03     |
| 28th  | 04.59   | 17.52     | 11.55   | —         |
| 29th  | 06.15   | 18.56     | 00.33   | 13.19     |
| 30th  | 07.15   | 19.49     | 01.53   | 14.24     |

# A SEA SHANTY FOR NOVEMBER

## The Fishes

A sea shanty for the salmon migration taking place around the coast and up the rivers this month. This is a tops'l halyard shanty, used when the rope (the halyard) that raised a topsail needed to be hauled, hence its simple rhythmic nature.

I'll sing you a song of the fish o' the sea and trust that you'll join in th[e] cho-rus with me, With a stor-my old wea-ther the stor-my old sea and when the wind blows you'll heave with me!

There once was a skipper, I don't know his name,
But I know that he played a very smart game.
*With a stormy old weather the stormy old sea*
*And when the wind blows you'll heave with me!*

When his ship lay becalmed in the tropical sea,
He whistled all day but he could get no breeze.
*With a stormy...*

Up leaped a salmon as bright as the sun,
He jumped between decks and then fired off a gun.
*With a stormy...*

Then came the eel with his slippery tail,
He climbed up aloft and he cast off each sail.
*With a stormy...*

The mackerel came then with his pretty striped back,
He hailed aft each sheet, and he boarded each tack.
*With a stormy...*

Then came the whale who was biggest at sea,
Shouting 'Haul in yer head sheets, now, hellums a-lee!'
*With a stormy...*

Then came the sprat, he was smallest of all,
He jumped on the poop cryin' 'Maintawps'l haul!'
*With a stormy...*

Last came the herring, the King of the Sea,
He looked at the men and said 'Captain I'll be!'
*With a stormy...*

The breeze it blew hard, and they sailed 'cross the sea,
Oh, what a smart captain that captain must be!
*With a stormy...*

N

# THE GARDEN

## November garden meditation

It is all death and decay in the garden now, but there are many incidental wonders as life fades away. Look for the dying stems draped elegantly over the edge of a pot, or the tinges of gold, ochre and umber in the trees, or the fuzz of almost neon moss against a chocolate-brown, rain-soaked log. Look for beauty and you will still find it in this swan song of a month.

Feel the cooling of the earth for yourself by stepping onto the soil barefoot for five minutes. While you do so, think about the great network of fungal mycelium spreading out beneath the soles of your feet. It is always there, but this is its moment of glory, as autumn rains signal that it is time for fungi to produce their fruiting bodies – mushrooms and toadstools to you and me. Look for them popping up in the base of hedges, in the lawn, under a tree, and appreciate that they are one tiny, showy tip of a massive iceberg below you.

Embrace the coming dark, and the cold. Allow yourself to feel the rain on your face and for your fingers to tingle with cold. Know that this season of closing down and resting is needed, and that it won't last for ever.

## Jobs in the garden

- Collect fallen leaves and put them into their own separate compost bin (or tip them all into a plastic bin bag poked with holes). Water them, and leave them for at least a year to rot down into beautiful leaf mould.
- Plant fruit bushes and trees. You can buy them as bare root trees now and they will establish very well over winter.
- Buy 'pot feet' for your terracotta containers to lift them away from the ground and allow them to drain well through winter rains and frosts.

## How much to sow

It is tempting to sow whole packets of seeds and then be overwhelmed by seedlings or, later, great gluts of one type of vegetable. This guide will help you to sow roughly the amount you need for a family of four; adjust to suit your own circumstances and favourites. In every case, sow a small number more than suggested to allow for non-germination and seedling failure.

**Garlic:** There is very little to sow this month but if you haven't planted out garlic you can still do so (three bulbs/thirty cloves).

**Broad beans:** If you haven't yet sown these, you can still do so: sow two 3-m rows.

**Peas:** If you have a polytunnel or large greenhouse, you could sow a 2-m row of hardy peas.

**Marrowfat peas:** Indoors, thickly sow a seedtray to cut a few weeks later as pea tips.

N

# THE KITCHEN

### Romani recipe for November – Bacon-fried trout

This is a simple way of cooking using ingredients Romanies would likely have to hand – flour, milk and bacon fat – and which would work well with most fish. Recipe based on the research of Romani and Traveller historian Robert Dawson.

Gut, clean and descale your trout. Dip in milk, then flour. Fry slowly in bacon fat.

### In season

### In the hedgerows, woods and fields
**Wild greens:** Chickweed, hairy bittercress, dandelion leaves, sow thistle, wintercress, sorrel
**Wild fruits and nuts:** Bullace, crab apple, haws, juniper berries, rosehips, rowan berries, sloes, sweet chestnuts, walnuts, wild damson
**Fungi:** Ceps, chanterelles, field mushrooms, horse mushrooms, common puffballs, parasols, shaggy inkcaps
**Roots:** Alexanders, dandelion, horseradish, Jerusalem artichoke, lovage, rampion, wild garlic
**Game:** Grouse, hare, pheasant, ptarmigan, rabbit, snipe, venison, grey squirrel, woodcock, mallard, partridge

### From the seashore and rivers
**Fish and shellfish:** Black bream, herring, oysters, turbot, mussels, brill, sardine, skate, clams, mussels

### From the kitchen garden
**Vegetables:** Jerusalem artichokes, cabbages, cardoon, carrots, celeriac, celery, chard, chicory, endive, kale, leeks, lettuce, onions, spring onions, shallots, Oriental leaves, parsnips, potatoes, pumpkins, winter squash, salsify, scorzonera, spinach, swede, turnips

**Fruits:** Quinces, medlars, pears
**Herbs:** Chervil, parsley, coriander, sage, rosemary, bay

**From the farms**
Goose

**And traditional imports**
Vacherin Mont d'Or, Beaujolais nouveau, truffles, cranberries,
satsumas, clementines, pomegranates

# RECIPES

### Cream of mushroom soup with green sauce and rosemary croutons

This is the month of mushrooms, but don't go out foraging unless you absolutely know your ceps and your girolles from your death caps and your funeral bells. You can make this soup with ordinary field mushrooms and add in some dried porcini for a wilder flavour, gathered for you by the experts.

| Serves 4–6 |
| --- |
| **Ingredients** |
| *For the soup* |
| 50g dried porcini |
| 50g butter |
| 1 onion, finely diced |
| 400g mushrooms, roughly chopped |
| 1 garlic clove, crushed |
| 850ml stock |
| 200ml double cream |
| |
| *For the green sauce* |
| Leaves from a large bunch of flat-leaved parsley |
| 60g blanched and toasted hazelnuts |
| 60g Parmesan cheese, finely grated |
| 150ml extra virgin olive oil |
| Juice of quarter of a lemon |
| Salt and pepper |

### For the croutons

6 tablespoons extra virgin olive oil

Sprig of rosemary

4 thick slices white bread, crusts removed, cut into cubes

## Method

To make the soup, put the porcini into a bowl, boil some water and pour over just enough to cover them, then leave to soak for 15 minutes. Heat the butter in a frying pan and sauté the onion for 5 minutes. Add the mushrooms and sauté until softened and starting to brown. Finally add the garlic and the drained porcini (reserving the juices) and cook for a few minutes. Transfer to a saucepan and add the stock and the reserved juices. Simmer for 20 minutes. Remove from the heat and use a hand-held blender to blitz smooth. Pass through a sieve, then return to the pot, add the cream and season with salt and pepper.

To make the green sauce, put all of the sauce ingredients into a food processor and whizz together.

To make the croutons, pour the olive oil into a frying pan. Pull the leaves from the rosemary, chop roughly and add to the pan, gently frying them for a few minutes to release their oils. Tip in the bread cubes and turn them until all of the oil has been absorbed by the bread, then fry for about 10 minutes, turning occasionally, until the croutons are toasty and coated.

When you are ready to serve, gently reheat the soup and pour into bowls, topping with a spoonful of the green sauce and a scattering of croutons.

N

GLEBE

KILMARTIN

NETHER LARGIE NORTH

NETHER LARGIE MID

TEMPLEWOOD

NETHER LARGIE SOUTH

RICRUIN

A MAP OF
KILMARTIN GLEN,
SCOTLAND .

# PILGRIMAGE OF THE MONTH

## Kilmartin Glen for St Andrew's Day

Celebrate the feast day of St Andrew, the patron saint of Scotland, with a pilgrimage to the Mull of Kintyre, which styles itself the ancient cradle of Scotland. At its northern end sits remote Kilmartin Glen, surrounded by wooded hills and distant mountain peaks. But this quiet backwater may once have been the original capital of Scotland and may fall along a 'ley line', an ancient druidical pilgrimage route. The glen (a narrow, deep valley) contains the greatest concentration of Neolithic and Bronze Age monuments in mainland Scotland – more than 800 within a 10-km radius.

Among the monuments is Dunadd, an ancient hillfort built on a craggy outcrop, where the kings of Dál Riata were inaugurated. Dál Riata was a Gaelic kingdom that straddled the North Channel (the strait between Northern Ireland and Scotland) in the 6th and 7th centuries, covering the western seaboard of Scotland, the Inner Hebrides and a chunk of Northern Ireland. The people of Dál Riata later became known as the Scotti, or Scoti, and gave Scotland its name. Kilmartin Glen was therefore once a great centre of activity, commerce and religious ritual. Though it seems ridiculously remote now for such important goings-on, it lies on a major land route between the inland lochs of western Scotland and the Irish Sea, linking mainland Scotland to religious centres such as nearby Iona and to Ireland and the rest of northern Europe.

A major feature of the valley is the 'Linear Cemetery', a row of five burial cairns stretching over nearly 5km. Their linear alignment has led to claims that the burial cairns were built along a ley line, one of many invisible straight lines that are said by some to crisscross Britain and Ireland. Ley lines were believed to be imbued with a mystical power, or 'earth energy', and may have been used as ancient pilgrimage routes. Along these routes, standing stones, wayside crosses, hillforts and ancient churches appear in astonishingly accurate

N

alignment, whether by coincidence, meticulous planning by the ancients or something more mysterious. The most famous are the St Michael's Line, running like an arrow between St Michael's Mount in Cornwall and Hopton-on-Sea in Norfolk and touching a multitude of ancient sites devoted to St Michael on its way; and the Belinus Line, running between Lee-on-the-Solent in Hampshire and Lairg in Scotland.

Kilmartin Glen's row of ancient burial cairns includes Glebe Cairn, 35m long and 3m high, dating from 1700BCE; Nether Largie North Cairn, which can be entered and where a stone cist (coffin) and stone carvings still lie; and chambered Nether Largie South Cairn, from 3000BCE. As though that weren't enough, a short distance away from the Linear Cemetery are ancient stone circles and rows of standing stones. Kilmartin Glen is a place worthy of a pilgrimage to pay homage to Scotland's past.

# MIGRATION OF THE MONTH

### The Atlantic run

Up Scottish rivers such as the Spey, the Tay, the Dee and the Tweed, and the Tyne in northeast England, come the silvery Atlantic salmon this month and next, as they return to the gravel beds of their birth. The time (up to four years) they've spent in the oceanic feeding grounds north of the Arctic Circle has meant they are in tiptop condition for the journey. As they arrive in the estuaries, they are met by fresh water, which immediately alters their bodies: they switch from using their longitudinal red muscles, which are useful for long-distance ocean swimming, to using their diagonally oriented white muscles, for thrashing from side to side. This gives them the power to leap up waterfalls and push against the current. They also darken in colour and the males develop strong jaws for fighting off other males when they reach the spawning grounds.

The salmon's homing instinct is uncanny, and the majority will return to the exact stream of their birth. They have an incredible sense of smell, and it is thought that each stream and river has its own scent and that it is this the salmon follow, catching a whiff of it in the estuaries and following it upstream.

Once they arrive at the spawning grounds, a female will select a 'riffle', an area of shallow water that flows fast and relatively turbulently over the gravel. She uses her tail to create a shallow depression, called a 'redd', where the eggs can nestle out of the current, and lays up to five thousand eggs into it. A male approaches and deposits his sperm into the redd, and the female covers the fertilised eggs by disturbing the gravel on the upstream edge of the redd. She then moves further upstream and creates another redd. This process is repeated up to seven times until all of her eggs are used up.

Spawned salmon only rarely return to the sea. The longer they are out of sea water, the more they deteriorate, and they nearly always die soon after spawning. The eggs will hatch after a few months and the small fish will live and feed in the river for up to three years before making their journey out to sea.

N

DECEMBER

MY GOD'S MONTH

ME-DEBLESKO MUNTHOS

XII

# December

 Start of meteorological winter

 Winter solstice, start of astronomical winter

 Yule/Midwinter/Midwinter's Day (pagan/neopagan/traditional)

 Christmas Eve (Christian)

 Christmas Day (Christian)

 Boxing Day/St Stephen's Day (Christian)

 New Year's Eve

# ROMANI NAME FOR THE MONTH

### Me-deblesko munthos – my god's month

The Romani name for December is a clear reference to Christmas and the birth of Jesus. There is no single religion within Romani culture, and depending on where they have travelled, some Romanies have adopted Islam and others have retained a faith in Hinduism that they may have brought with them from roots in India. But the vast majority are Christians, and almost all British and Irish Romanies are.

The Christian Romanies have their own patron saint, St Sarah, also known as Sara-la-Kali. One account says that Sarah was the Egyptian maid of one of the Three Marys, who arrived in the Camargue in southern France in a boat to escape early Christian persecution. Another says that she was a chief of her Romanichal tribe in the Rhone, and had a vision that the saints who had been present at the death of Jesus would come to shore, and that she must help them. When she saw the Three Marys arriving, she turned her cloak miraculously into a raft and sailed out to meet them. Either way, a great pilgrimage is made by Romanies from all over Europe to Saintes-Maries-de-la-Mer to honour her on 24th May each year, when her statue is carried into the water there.

This month Romani families would have hunkered down for the winter, perhaps tucked into the lee of a hedgerow sparkling with frost, with a glowing fire to gather around and warm cold hands and feet, its smoke wafting through the chilly air. The men might work at hedge laying and dry-stone walling, depending on the part of the country, and the women and children would gather mistletoe and make holly wreaths to sell at the markets ahead of Christmas. And when the day came, a full roast dinner would be cooked outdoors over the fire – goose, pudding and all.

# THE MOON

## Moon phases

New moon – 4th December, 07.43

1st quarter – 11th December, 01.36

Full moon – 19th December, 04.36*

3rd quarter – 27th December, 02.24

## Gardening by the moon

**3rd quarter to new moon: 1st–4th and 27th–31st.** Prune. Harvest for storage. Fertilise and mulch the soil.

**New moon to 1st quarter: 4th–11th.** Sow crops that develop below ground. Dig the soil.

**1st quarter to full moon: 11th–19th.** Sow crops that develop above ground. Plant seedlings and young plants.

**Full moon to 3rd quarter: 19th–27th.** Harvest crops for immediate eating. Harvest fruit.

## Moon sign – Sagittarius

Astrologers believe that the new moon is a time to make plans and focus on your dreams and hopes for the period ahead, and that each new moon has a particular energy, depending on which zodiacal sign it is in. The new moon on the 4th will be in Sagittarius, which is said to be a freedom-loving sign, making this a good time to plan travel and to think about how to release some of the bonds holding you.

*This month the full moon falls in the early hours of the morning. To see the moon at its fullest within normal waking hours, view it the evening before the date given above.

### Navigating by the stars, sun and moon

### Find due west and east using Mintaka

For some really precise celestial navigation we can look again
to Orion, that great winter constellation that is so clear and
prominent in our skies now, rising earlier and earlier each
night. Look in particular to Mintaka, the right-hand star in
Orion's belt. Mintaka – the name comes from *mantaqa*, an
Arabic term for 'belt' – is actually a multiple star system 1,200
light years from the sun. Very usefully for our navigational
purposes, Mintaka rises almost precisely due west and sets
almost precisely due east. Orion will rise at around 19.00 at
the beginning of December, and by the end of the month will
be rising as the sun sets, if you would like to look out for it.

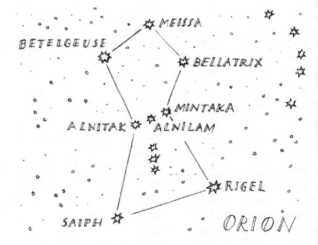

## Moon rise and set

| | St Michael's Mount | | Hopton-on-Sea | | |
|---|---|---|---|---|---|
| | Rise | Set | Rise | Set | |
| 1st | 03.52 | 14.53 | 03.25 | 14.20 | |
| 2nd | 05.18 | 15.15 | 04.54 | 14.38 | |
| 3rd | 06.48 | 15.43 | 06.27 | 15.02 | |
| 4th | 08.18 | 16.21 | 08.01 | 15.37 | new moon |
| 5th | 09.42 | 17.13 | 09.28 | 16.27 | |
| 6th | 10.51 | 18.21 | 10.37 | 17.34 | |
| 7th | 11.42 | 19.40 | 11.27 | 18.56 | |
| 8th | 12.18 | 21.03 | 12.00 | 20.21 | |
| 9th | 12.45 | 22.23 | 12.24 | 21.45 | |
| 10th | 13.05 | 23.40 | 12.41 | 23.05 | |
| 11th | 13.21 | — | 12.55 | — | 1st quarter |
| 12th | 13.36 | 00.53 | 13.07 | 00.21 | |
| 13th | 13.50 | 02.04 | 13.19 | 01.34 | |
| 14th | 14.05 | 03.13 | 13.32 | 02.46 | |
| 15th | 14.22 | 04.22 | 13.46 | 03.58 | |
| 16th | 14.42 | 05.31 | 14.03 | 05.10 | |
| 17th | 15.06 | 06.40 | 14.25 | 06.21 | |
| 18th | 15.38 | 07.46 | 14.54 | 07.30 | |
| 19th | 16.19 | 08.48 | 15.33 | 08.34 | full moon |
| 20th | 17.10 | 09.42 | 16.24 | 09.28 | |
| 21st | 18.10 | 10.26 | 17.26 | 10.11 | |
| 22nd | 19.18 | 11.00 | 18.35 | 10.44 | |
| 23rd | 20.29 | 11.28 | 19.49 | 11.08 | |
| 24th | 21.42 | 11.49 | 21.05 | 11.28 | |
| 25th | 22.56 | 12.08 | 22.22 | 11.43 | |
| 26th | — | 12.24 | 23.40 | 11.57 | |
| 27th | 00.11 | 12.40 | — | 12.10 | 3rd quarter |
| 28th | 01.28 | 12.56 | 01.00 | 12.24 | |
| 29th | 02.49 | 13.15 | 02.23 | 12.40 | |
| 30th | 04.14 | 13.39 | 03.52 | 13.00 | |
| 31st | 05.42 | 14.10 | 05.23 | 13.28 | |

Where moonset times are before moonrise times, this is the setting of the previous night's moon.

# THE SKY

## At night

**1st:** Venus, Jupiter and Saturn all visible from about 16.30 in the south, and for the next two weeks or so.

**2nd:** Venus will be at its brightest tonight, though it is also bright for a week or so either side of this date. Visible from 16.00 in the dusk until setting at 18.00 in the south.

**7th:** Close approach of Venus and the moon, visible in the dusk from about 16.00 in the south, at an altitude of 13 degrees, until setting at 18.00 in the southwest.

## By day

**21st:** The winter solstice falls at 15.59, when the North Pole is at its maximum tilt away from the sun. At this moment the sun will be above the Tropic of Capricorn, which is the southernmost latitude at which the sun can be directly overhead. The word solstice comes from the Latin *solstitium*, which means 'sun stopping', as the position on the horizon at which the sun rises and sets stops and reverses direction today.

**21st:** At solar midday the sun reaches an altitude of 16 degrees at Lee-on-the-Solent in Hampshire and 9 degrees at Lairg in Scotland.

**1st:** Earliest sunrise, St Michael's Mount (07.59) and Hopton-on-Sea (07.41).

**1st:** Latest sunset, St Michael's Mount (16.22) and Hopton-on-Sea (15.42).

**1st–21st:** Daylight decreases by 0h 20m at St Michael's Mount and by 0h 23m at Hopton-on-Sea.

**21st–31st:** Daylight increases by 0h 5m at St Michael's Mount and by 0h 6m at Hopton-on-Sea.

## Sunrise and set

| | St Michael's Mount | | Hopton-on-Sea | |
|---|---|---|---|---|
| | Rise | Set | Rise | Set |
| 1st | 07.59 | 16.22 | 07.41 | 15.42 |
| 2nd | 08.00 | 16.21 | 07.42 | 15.41 |
| 3rd | 08.01 | 16.21 | 07.44 | 15.41 |
| 4th | 08.03 | 16.20 | 07.45 | 15.40 |
| 5th | 08.04 | 16.20 | 07.46 | 15.40 |
| 6th | 08.05 | 16.20 | 07.48 | 15.39 |
| 7th | 08.06 | 16.19 | 07.49 | 15.39 |
| 8th | 08.07 | 16.19 | 07.50 | 15.39 |
| 9th | 08.08 | 16.19 | 07.51 | 15.38 |
| 10th | 08.09 | 16.19 | 07.52 | 15.38 |
| 11th | 08.10 | 16.19 | 07.53 | 15.38 |
| 12th | 08.11 | 16.19 | 07.54 | 15.38 |
| 13th | 08.12 | 16.19 | 07.55 | 15.38 |
| 14th | 08.13 | 16.19 | 07.56 | 15.38 |
| 15th | 08.14 | 16.19 | 07.57 | 15.38 |
| 16th | 08.15 | 16.19 | 07.58 | 15.38 |
| 17th | 08.15 | 16.20 | 07.59 | 15.39 |
| 18th | 08.16 | 16.20 | 07.59 | 15.39 |
| 19th | 08.17 | 16.20 | 08.00 | 15.39 |
| 20th | 08.17 | 16.21 | 08.01 | 15.40 |
| 21st | 08.18 | 16.21 | 08.01 | 15.40 |
| 22nd | 08.18 | 16.22 | 08.02 | 15.41 |
| 23rd | 08.19 | 16.22 | 08.02 | 15.41 |
| 24th | 08.19 | 16.23 | 08.03 | 15.42 |
| 25th | 08.20 | 16.24 | 08.03 | 15.43 |
| 26th | 08.20 | 16.24 | 08.03 | 15.43 |
| 27th | 08.20 | 16.25 | 08.03 | 15.44 |
| 28th | 08.20 | 16.26 | 08.03 | 15.45 |
| 29th | 08.20 | 16.27 | 08.04 | 15.46 |
| 30th | 08.20 | 16.28 | 08.04 | 15.47 |
| 31st | 08.20 | 16.29 | 08.04 | 15.48 |

# THE SEA

## Average sea temperature

| | |
|---|---|
| Orkney: | 9.1°C |
| South Shields: | 9.1°C |
| Carrickfergus: | 10.5°C |
| Lowestoft: | 9.7°C |
| Aberystwyth: | 10.8°C |
| Bantry: | 11.1°C |
| Cowes: | 11.8°C |
| Penzance: | 11.7°C |

## Spring and neap tides

The spring tides are the most extreme tides of the month, with the highest rises and falls, and the neap tides are the least extreme, with the smallest. Exact timings vary around the coast, but expect them around the following dates:

**Spring tides:** 4th–5th and 20th–21st

**Neap tides:** 12th–13th and 27th–28th

In the tide timetable opposite, spring tides are shown with an asterisk.

**December tide timetable for Dover**

For guidance on how to convert this for your local area, see page 8.

|  | *High water* | | *Low water* | |
|---|---|---|---|---|
|  | Morning | Afternoon | Morning | Afternoon |
| 1st | 08.06 | 20.36 | 02.54 | 15.21 |
| 2nd | 08.54 | 21.20 | 03.49 | 16.16 |
| 3rd | 09.39 | 22.05 | 04.42 | 17.10 |
| 4th | 10.25 | 22.50 | 05.34 | 18.02* |
| 5th | 11.11 | 23.36 | 06.23 | 18.51* |
| 6th | 11.59 | — | 07.12 | 19.39 |
| 7th | 00.24 | 12.49 | 08.00 | 20.25 |
| 8th | 01.15 | 13.43 | 08.49 | 21.13 |
| 9th | 02.08 | 14.41 | 09.40 | 22.03 |
| 10th | 03.05 | 15.43 | 10.36 | 22.59 |
| 11th | 04.05 | 16.53 | 11.36 | — |
| 12th | 05.10 | 18.11 | 00.02 | 12.41 |
| 13th | 06.24 | 19.23 | 01.08 | 13.46 |
| 14th | 07.32 | 20.19 | 02.12 | 14.48 |
| 15th | 08.28 | 21.04 | 03.12 | 15.44 |
| 16th | 09.15 | 21.45 | 04.04 | 16.30 |
| 17th | 09.58 | 22.22 | 04.49 | 17.09 |
| 18th | 10.36 | 22.57 | 05.27 | 17.43 |
| 19th | 11.10 | 23.31 | 06.00 | 18.15 |
| 20th | 11.42 | — | 06.33 | 18.48* |
| 21st | 00.03 | 12.13 | 07.06 | 19.21* |
| 22nd | 00.32 | 12.41 | 07.41 | 19.55 |
| 23rd | 01.00 | 13.12 | 08.17 | 20.31 |
| 24th | 01.33 | 13.47 | 08.55 | 21.08 |
| 25th | 02.13 | 14.31 | 09.35 | 21.49 |
| 26th | 03.01 | 15.24 | 10.21 | 22.36 |
| 27th | 03.59 | 16.32 | 11.16 | 23.36 |
| 28th | 05.08 | 17.53 | — | 12.23 |
| 29th | 06.21 | 19.04 | 00.51 | 13.35 |
| 30th | 07.27 | 20.05 | 02.05 | 14.40 |
| 31st | 08.26 | 21.00 | 03.12 | 15.44 |

# A SEA SHANTY FOR DECEMBER

**Rolling Home**

One of many superstitions attached to shantying was that songs about setting out should be sung only on the outward journey and songs about coming home only on the inward one. This forebitter (a song sung in the sailors' leisure time) sees our sailors starting for home from Australia, sailing right around the world, and eventually being lit along the south coast and into port by the lighthouses of the Lizard, Start Point, Eddystone, Portland Bill and Dover. A fitting end to our year of shanties.

To Australia's lovely daughters,
We will bid a fond adieu,
For we're bound for dear Old England
To return no more to you.
*Rolling home, rolling home,*
*Rolling home across the sea,*
*Rolling home to dear Old England,*
*Rolling home, fair land, to thee.*

Up aloft amidst the rigging
Blows the wild and rushing gale,
Straining every spar and backstay,
Spreading out each swelling sail.
*Rolling home...*

Cheer up, Jack, bright smiles await you
From the fairest of the fair,
There are loving hearts to greet you
With kind welcomes everywhere.
*Rolling home...*

And we'll sing the joyful chorus
In the watches of the night,
And we'll see the shores of England
When the grey dawn brings the light.
*Rolling home...*

D

# THE GARDEN

## December garden meditation

Everything is sleeping in the garden now: mammals tucked away, perennial plants died back to their roots, insects snoozing in hollow stems or piles of dry leaves. Step into your garden and sense the peace, the slumber, and think about the fact that your garden needs this period of deep rest. You can almost hear the snoring. We are at the darkest end of the year, when there is so much more night than day, making this a good time to take your five-minute meditation as night falls. Look up at the stars and think about how the piece of earth on which you stand is now tipped away from the sun and towards the dark and the cold, and that this is the reason frosts form and snowflakes fall. Look up into eternity.

But know also as you gaze into the endless dark and cold that we are at the turning point of the year. After the winter solstice this month, the northern hemisphere will start to slowly tip back towards our warm, welcoming, life-giving sun. The garden, the creatures and the plants will immediately sense it and within weeks will start to rouse themselves. So this point in the year may be the darkest, but it is a moment for great hope and rejoicing. It all gets lighter after this.

## Jobs in the garden

- Keep bird feeders topped up and provide fresh water in a bird bath. Check on frozen mornings that there is plenty of thawed water. Throw out chopped-up apples for the fieldfares and redwings.
- Cut stems of berried evergreens for Christmas decoration at the beginning of the month and store them in vases of water in a shed, porch or sheltered corner of the garden.
- Prune grapevines while they are dormant. Their sap starts to flow early in the new year.

## How much to sow

It is tempting to sow whole packets of seeds and then be overwhelmed by seedlings or, later, great gluts of one type of vegetable. This guide will help you to sow roughly the amount you need for a family of four; adjust to suit your own circumstances and favourites. In every case, sow a small number more than suggested to allow for non-germination and seedling failure.

**Garlic:** There is very little to sow in December but you can still plant garlic if you didn't do it earlier (three bulbs of different varieties).

**Broadbeans:** You can also still plant broadbeans indoors if you didn't manage to sow any outdoors in October or November. About 30 plants.

# MIGRATION OF THE MONTH

### Redwings

By December most travellers have found a place to hunker down and will not be on the move until spring. There are few migrations in midwinter, for the obvious reason that most creatures migrate in autumn specifically to find a place to sit out this dark and chilly bit. However, a blast of icy weather, should one hit, can put some birds on the move again.

Redwings carried out their main migration back in October. Coming from Russia and Scandinavia, they gathered along the Scandinavian coast and then set off as night fell, completing the 800-km journey across the North Sea in one great flight. They stick together, travelling in flocks, sometimes mixing with fieldfares – other winter migrants who behave in a similar way.

Their first call on reaching Britain and Ireland is the orchards and hedgerows, feasting on leftover fruits, and as winter goes on they take to open farmland and dig for worms among the stubble. But when snow and ice hit, they will move again. After a heavy snowfall, city dwellers may open their curtains to see not just a newly soft and white version of their garden, but also a great flock of redwings and fieldfares perched in a nearby tree. The birds spend these cold winter spells in cities because they are warmer than the open countryside and because there are greater opportunities to find food, once autumn's bounty has been gobbled up. Give them fruits and berries, a treat of mealworms and some unfrozen water if you want to help them keep going. When the temperature rises again, they will head back to the countryside. Come spring, they migrate back across the North Sea to their breeding grounds in Scandinavia and beyond, their brief but crucial sojourn in our gardens long behind them.

# THE KITCHEN

### Romani recipe for December – Gypsy stuffing and chicken roll

A stuffing to use as part of a Romani Christmas feast, cooked on an outdoor fire, or as a part of this chicken dish. Recipe based on the research of Romani and Traveller historian Robert Dawson.

Mince 400g fatty bacon with 800g pork. Mix in 2 eggs, chopped onion, rosemary and sage, breadcrumbs and garlic, then season with salt and pepper. To use as it is, bake in a buttered ovenproof dish at 190°C/Gas Mark 5 for 50 minutes – 1 hour. Or to use the stuffing in a chicken roll, lay out a boned chicken, spread the uncooked stuffing over it, roll up and wrap in foil. Cook for 2 ½ hours at 180°C/Gas Mark 4 or in a Dutch oven over a low heat.

### In season

### In the hedgerows, woods and fields
**Wild greens:** Chickweed, hairy bittercress, dandelion leaves, sow thistle, wintercress
**Wild fruits and nuts:** Crab apple, sweet chestnuts
**Roots:** Alexanders, dandelion, horseradish, Jerusalem artichoke, lovage, rampion, wild garlic
**Game:** Hare, pheasant, rabbit, snipe, venison, woodcock

### From the seashore and rivers
**Fish and shellfish:** Mussels, oysters, turbot, black bream, herring

### From the kitchen garden
**Vegetables:** As for November (see page 234), plus Brussels sprouts will be ready after the first frost
**Fruits:** Quinces
**Herbs:** Chervil, parsley, coriander, sage, rosemary, bay

### From the farms
Stilton, goose, turkey

### And traditional imports
Vacherin Mont d'Or, truffles, cranberries, satsumas, clementines, pomegranates

# RECIPES

### Feast of the Seven Fishes pie

There is a southern Italian tradition to eat seven different types of fish on Christmas Eve, because it is considered a 'fast day' when no meat can be eaten, ahead of the feast day of Christmas Day itself. Usually the meal would consist of a great array of individual dishes – a proper feast – but if that feels a bit too much to manage on Christmas Eve, make this Feast of the Seven Fishes pie instead, which has a fragrant and saffron-tinged tomato sauce rather than the white sauce of a traditional fisherman's pie. You can obviously choose fish to suit availability and your own tastes, as long as the total adds up to seven.

| |
|---|
| **Serves 8** |
| **Ingredients** |
| 2 pinches saffron |
| 200ml olive oil |
| 2 fennel bulbs, diced |
| 2 red peppers, diced |
| 3 × 400g tins chopped plum tomatoes |
| 30g tomato purée |
| Zest and juice of 1 orange |
| ½ teaspoon fennel seeds |
| 2 bay leaves |
| 125g all butter puff pastry |
| 200g each of 5 different fish, perhaps cod, monkfish, red mullet, John Dory and gurnard |
| 125g jar pickled mussels, drained |
| 150g prawns |
| 1 beaten egg |
| Salt and pepper |

## Method

Preheat the oven to 180°C/Gas Mark 4. Put the saffron in a
bowl and pour on just enough boiling water to cover it. Heat
the olive oil in a large saucepan over a low to medium heat
and stir in the fennel. Cook for a few minutes then add the red
pepper and continue until both are softened. Tip in the chopped
tomatoes, tomato purée, orange zest and juice, fennel seeds and
bay leaves, plus the saffron in its water. Allow to bubble gently
for 10–15 minutes.

For the pastry lid, roll out the pastry on a floured surface
to the size of the top of your ovenproof dish, and set aside.

Remove the sauce from the heat. Cut the fish into bite-
sized pieces and add it to the sauce, then stir in the mussels and
prawns. Add a little boiling water if needed to cover the fish, and
bring back to the boil. Season with salt and pepper, and tip it
into your ovenproof dish.

Place the pastry lid on top. Paint it with the beaten egg
and use the offcuts to decorate the top if you are feeling fancy,
painting them too. Otherwise, just make a hole in the top to
allow some of the steam to escape when cooking. Bake for
20–25 minutes or until the top is nicely risen and browned.

### Spiced apricot and orange creams with pistachio, pomegranate and dark chocolate

A dessert that manages to feel Christmassy without the slightest whiff of mincemeat. The creams can be made several days ahead and stored in the fridge for whipping out and decorating at the last minute.

**Serves 4**

**Ingredients**

300g dried apricots

1 cinnamon stick

3 cloves

1–2 glasses white wine

3 leaves gelatine

55ml full fat milk

275ml fromage frais

30g golden caster sugar

*For topping*

50g dark chocolate

50g pistachios, chopped lengthwise

Seeds of half a pomegranate

**Method**

Line 4 teacups with clingfilm, and then lightly grease the insides with a flavourless oil such as sunflower oil.

Put the apricots into a saucepan with the cinnamon stick and cloves and enough white wine to cover them. Bring to the boil, and simmer for 10 minutes. Leave to cool. Remove the spices and drain the apricots, reserving the liquid. Use a hand-held blender to blitz them smooth, adding a few splashes of the reserved liquid if needed to make a spoonable purée.

Put the gelatine in a bowl, cover with water, and leave to soak for 5 minutes. Heat the milk in a saucepan. Remove the gelatine from the water, squeezing out the excess liquid, then add it to the milk and whisk it – it will quickly dissolve. Pour this into a mixing bowl with the fruit purée, fromage frais and sugar, and mix well. Divide between the 4 teacups and cover with clingfilm or saucers. Refrigerate for a few hours or, ideally, overnight.

For the topping, melt the chocolate in a dish over hot water. Turn the creams out into individual bowls, drizzle with the chocolate and sprinkle with the pistachios and pomegranate seeds.

D

STONEHENGE

PROCESSIONAL AVENUE

← ROUTE OF A303 →

W

A MAP OF
STONEHENGE

# PILGRIMAGE OF THE MONTH

## Stonehenge for Midwinter

Stonehenge is England's great Stone Age cathedral, erected around 2500BCE in the late Neolithic period. It is an extremely complex and intricate structure, and when complete worked both as lunar and solar calendar and as eclipse predictor. But who built it and exactly what they used it for have been the subject of fierce debate. Despite this, archaeological evidence suggests that it was always a place of pilgrimage and somewhere that Neolithic people would travel great distances to reach, in order to gather, dance, get married, trade goods, share information and observe the heavens. In particular, Stonehenge was a place to mark the key moments in the astronomical year: the summer and winter solstices at midsummer and midwinter.

And this continues today. Now, at the summer solstice, great gatherings of about ten thousand people come to party, meditate, worship and watch the sun rise, which today occurs just to the left of the Heel Stone. (It is thought originally to have had a partner stone, so that the sun would have been framed between them.) At the winter solstice, the sun would have set exactly opposite the position of the midsummer sunrise, framed between the two uprights of the tallest trilithon (two large vertical stones supporting a third, horizontal one), though half of one upright has now fallen. In fact, it seems likely that it was midwinter that saw the major gatherings in ancient times, and it is the midwinter sunset that can be viewed through these stones from the processional avenue leading up to it. Although Stonehenge is fenced off for most of the year, it is opened for midsummer, midwinter and the equinoxes, when you can visit and get in among the vast and ancient stones.

Stonehenge predates the Iron Age, the time of the druids, but modern druids who have revived the religion feel a strong connection with Stonehenge and a kinship with the ancient astronomers who built the stones. They make their pilgrimages to it and make use of it for their own rituals marking these moments upon which the year turns.

# REFERENCES

Astronomical and calendarial information reproduced with
   permission from HM Nautical Almanac Office (HMNAO),
   UK Hydrographic Office (UKHO) and the Controller of Her
   Majesty's Stationery Office

Moon and sun rises and sets and further calculations reproduced
   with permission from www.timeanddate.com

Tidal predictions reproduced with permission from HMNAO,
   UKHO and the Controller of Her Majesty's Stationery Office

Astronomical events are based on ephemerides obtained using the
   NASA JPL Horizons system

Sea temperatures are reproduced with permission from
   www.seatemperature.org

# FURTHER READING

Dawson, Robert, *An English to Romany/Scottish/Irish Traveller
   Dictionary*, Blackwell, Derbyshire, published by Robert Dawson,
   2009

Gogerty, Clare, *Beyond the Footpath: Mindful Adventures for
   Modern Pilgrims*, London: Piatkus, 2019

Hugill, Stan, *Shanties from the Seven Seas*, Mystic, CT: Mystic
   Seaport Museum Stores, 1994

Hutton, Ronald, *The Stations of the Sun: a History of the Ritual
   Year in Britain*, Oxford: Oxford University Press, 1996

Le Bas, Damian, *The Stopping Places: A Journey Through Gypsy
   Britain*, London: Chatto & Windus, 2018

Newman, Hugh and others, *Megalith: Studies in Stone*, Glastonbury,
   Somerset: Wooden Books, 2018

Nozedar, Adele, *The Hedgerow Handbook: Recipes, Remedies and
   Rituals*, London: Square Peg, 2012

Sampson, John, *The Dialect of the Gypsies of Wales*, Oxford: Oxford
   University Press, 1968 (originally published 1926)

Smith-Bendell, Maggie, *Our Forgotten Years: A Gypsy Woman's Life
   on the Road*, Hatfield: University of Hertfordshire Press, 2009

Sullivan, Danny, *Leys: Secret Spirit Paths in Ancient Britain*,
   Glastonbury, Somerset: Wooden Books, 2005

The British Pilgrimage Trust, britishpilgrimage.org

# ACKNOWLEDGEMENTS

Thank you to everyone who has helped me to create this almanac.

Special thanks to Damian Le Bas and Robert Dawson for their insights into the Romani way of life and guidance on recipes, language and the Romani year. It has been a real privilege to have this glimpse into such a hidden way of life. Thanks also to Damian's nan, Julie Jones, née Ayres, for contributing her recipe for rasher pudding.

Huge thanks to Richard Barnard who has again taken suggestions for songs and meticulously researched and put his own spin on them before making them *Almanac*-ready. Your creative and careful work is hugely appreciated. Thanks again also to my dad, Jack Leendertz, who takes care of the 'Sky at night' sections so brilliantly and diligently each year.

Thanks to Adele Nozedar for permission to use your sugared damson recipe, to Ellen Hughes for your samphire recipe inspiration and to Chris Hewson at the British Trust for Ornithology for swift advice. Thank you to Alice Attlee and Guy Hayward of the British Pilgrimage Trust for putting up with all of my pestering, and to Clare Gogerty for your wonderful and inspirational pilgrimage book and for being so generous with your help. Belated thanks also to Adam Robertson who helped me with the 2020 edition and who I forgot to thank! The benefit of creating an annual publication…

It has been a joy working with illustrator Helen Cann, chosen for her mastery of maps in this very map-based edition but who has taken the brief and run with it so creatively, making such magical and characterful work. Thank you, Helen.

Thanks to my son, Rowan Simpson, for taking some of the gruelling data input work off of my hands. Good to have you apprenticed into the family business.

Huge thanks as ever to the wonderful team who put *The Almanac* together: Matt Cox of Newman+Eastwood, Stephanie Jackson, Jonathan Christie, Ella Parsons, Matt Grindon, Karen Baker, Kevin Hawkins, Alison Wormleighton and Jane Birch. Thanks also, of course, to my agent, Adrian Sington at Kruger Cowne.

Thanks to my mum, Cath Read, and stepdad, John Read, for logistical and emotional support always. And Rowan has already had a mention but biggest love and thanks always go to my gorgeous family, Michael, Rowan and Meg, just because.

# INDEX

## ABOUT THE AUTHOR

**Lia Leendertz** is an award-winning garden and food writer based in Bristol. Her reinvention of the traditional rural almanac has become an annual must-have for readers eager to connect with the seasons, appreciate the outdoors and discover ways to mark and celebrate each month. Now established as the bestselling almanac in the market, this is the fourth instalment.

**Find out more about Lia at:**
www.lialeendertz.com
@lialeendertz
@lia_leendertz

## ABOUT THE ILLUSTRATOR

**Helen Cann** is an award-winning illustrator, author and artist specialising in hand-drawn maps. Her work has been commissioned to appear in books, television and film. She has exhibited across the UK and also runs the occasional hand-drawn mapping workshop. She loves hiking in the South Downs near her home and is never without an old-school paper walking map...

**Find out more about Helen at:**
helencann.co.uk
@helen_cann
@helencannart

# CALENDAR 2021

## JULY

| M | T | W | T | F | S | S |
|---|---|---|---|---|---|---|
|   |   |   | 1 | 2 | 3 | 4 |
| 5 | 6 | 7 | 8 | 9 | 10 | 11 |
| 12 | 13 | 14 | 15 | 16 | 17 | 18 |
| 19 | 20 | 21 | 22 | 23 | 24 | 25 |
| 26 | 27 | 28 | 29 | 30 | 31 |   |

## SEPTEMBER

| M | T | W | T | F | S | S |
|---|---|---|---|---|---|---|
|   |   | 1 | 2 | 3 | 4 | 5 |
| 6 | 7 | 8 | 9 | 10 | 11 | 12 |
| 13 | 14 | 15 | 16 | 17 | 18 | 19 |
| 20 | 21 | 22 | 23 | 24 | 25 | 26 |
| 27 | 28 | 29 | 30 |   |   |   |

## NOVEMBER

| M | T | W | T | F | S | S |
|---|---|---|---|---|---|---|
| 1 | 2 | 3 | 4 | 5 | 6 | 7 |
| 8 | 9 | 10 | 11 | 12 | 13 | 14 |
| 15 | 16 | 17 | 18 | 19 | 20 | 21 |
| 22 | 23 | 24 | 25 | 26 | 27 | 28 |
| 29 | 30 |   |   |   |   |   |